# RED LIGHT DISTRICTS

# OF THE WORLD

Fiona Pitt-Kethley

**Tamworth Press**

First published in 2000
By Tamworth Press
© Fiona Pitt-Kethley 2000

A catalogue record for this book is available from the British Library.


Printed in Great Britain by Antony Rowe Ltd

ISBN 0 9509441 3 0


Tamworth Press

Cover photograph of Hamburg © Fiona Pitt-Kethley

# Acknowledgements

These essays were published first in slightly different forms in the following publications: *Forum, The Guardian (Ars Amatoria), The Scotsman, Scotland on Sunday* and *The Big Issue.*

I would like to thank the following for their help with my research as interpreters, mentors, bodyguards, and informants:

Bruce Meyer and "The Outlaw" in Toronto (1990)
Mischa de Vreede, Guus Luijters and "Batman" in Amsterdam (1990)
"Chris", the makers of *Nighthawks* and an anonymous taxi-driver in Dublin (1990)
Koji Sawada and Keith Haines in Japan (1991)
Moshe and 14 other fireman from Jerusalem, a doctor called Mostafa, an endocrinologist called Muhammad and the crew of The Nefertari in Egypt (1991 to 1992)
Daniel de Souza and Kaan Erge in Turkey (1992)
Philip Ditchfield in Athens (1992)
Zygmunt Frankel in Tel Aviv (1992)
Punters, professionals and sex-shop keepers in Brussels (1993)
César Roque Vazquez in Mexico City (1993)
Punters, professionals and sex shop-keepers in Copenhagen (1993)
Jürgen Brustkern in Berlin and Hamburg (1994)
Ron Hogan and Steve Feinberg in Los Angeles (1994)
Those who mugged me in Budapest (1994)
"Don" in Hong Kong who went way beyond the call of duty...(1994)

I would also like to thank all the other informants who begged me not to include their names and all those who wrote to me with ideas.

I would also like to acknowledge the help of the Society of Authors for an Arthur Welton bursary towards research expenses.

# Contents

# Preface

THIS BOOK OUGHT by right to be as long as the Encyclopaedia Britannica. Every country has its red-light districts and probably every single one of these has its own ambience and its own story. To contain even a partial survey within the pages of one volume I had to be selective. Finance too was a problem. A generous advance from a large publisher might have made it possible to visit enough places to produce a book as fat as the Bible.

The typescript of this book has been rejected by almost as many publishers as Golding's *Lord of the Flies*. Those that saw parts of this manuscript seemed to have a singularly strange attitude to it. A firm that is famous for religious books took my agent out to lunch, begged for a look at the book, than told him how shocked they were by the chapter on Amsterdam. Just what did they expect? A Bible in every brothel? In fact, most of the newspaper editors and publishers managed to hang on to the typescript while evincing great shock at its contents. The shock, if not religious, had more than a whiff of political correctness. One female editor criticised my "non-judgemental" attitude. Others returned it with one or more chapters missing, presumably those that covered the destination of their next business trip. Some even admitted they enjoyed it. "It's funny and informative, but I'm afraid I don't see how we could publish it" one wrote. He had enjoyed it so much that the edges of the pages were positively chewed and frothed upon. As a punishment to all such publishers I have deliberately not included any addresses that might be useful at the Frankfurt Book Fair.

At one stage I advertised for information in *The London Review of Books* and its readers were very helpful. I feel somewhat guilty that I did not manage, because of lack of money, to get to all the addresses they gave me. Some men would only volunteer information in person. I got good details from one famous actor over a pot of Lapsang Souchong. A journalist who had once been a travel courier gave me an even longer list over gin and ginger beer. I enjoyed his story of his revenge on a group of rude Huddersfield businessmen who had given him hell during a trip he was escorting. They wanted a hot spot for the night, so he sent them to a club where old ladies hunted for gigolos… "They were a very chastened lot on the plane next morning," he reminisced. That club was in Frankfurt, which was also the city where a tabloid newspaper editor suffered an unfortunate escapade with some British prostitutes who had turned up to service the Book Fair. He left the Jacuzzi with nothing but his trousers... He proudly told me the story over Rioja and whitebait.

Visiting brothels was an exceptionally odd hobby for a woman, but it has given me good after-dinner and lecture anecdotes. I am a past master, or mistress, at lowering the tone of any conversation and few of my listeners can resist listening to tales of Eastern technique or Western depravity, or vice versa. Entertaining as my red-light visits were though, there is a stage where almost anyone gets brothel-fatigue. I could, I suppose, have gone on with this book for years more at my own expense. When I decided to marry I toyed with the idea of a honeymoon in Bangkok. My husband could have stayed in the hotel while I went to the sex shows. It would have been a strange reversal of roles. But in the end I thought enough is enough. Bangkok has been thoroughly turned inside out by TV film crews. We all know those stories by heart. I am slightly sorrier that I did not visit the brothel in Australia where certain publishing executives are said to while the hours away. Conveniently it comes up on the company credit card as a bistro.

Now my days of watching strippers and live sex acts are numbered and I will probably never browse through bestiality videos again. I decided to settle down, marry, tend my allotment, have a baby and lead a relatively sober life. My brothel-creeping days are over. I leave visits to such places to my readers or any other brave soul who wants to continue my project and visit the uncharted red-light districts of the globe.

# Introduction

PROSTITUTION, "THE oldest profession", is omnipresent. However illegal a country makes it, it will surface somewhere. Prostitutes will masquerade as dancers, masseurs, models, escorts, etc. until most of these words become euphemisms for other activities. While prostitution is everywhere, red light districts have passed away in many countries for one of several reasons. During my researches I corresponded with friends and friends of friends throughout the world, before deciding which cities were worth visiting. Finland and Iceland, I learned, have comparatively little demand for prostitution. While the older and less attractive partner often ends up paying, transactions are on an *ad hoc* basis. In Finland, a financial offer on a discreetly folded piece of paper might be passed to the person next to you at the bar. In other countries red-light districts have faded away more from repression than free expression. While rich Arabs still patronise prostitutes, they are likely to do this in other countries or via a call-girl system. There is little public prostitution left in most of the Middle East.

Prostitution will always thrive while there are men to pay for it, but red-light districts are slowly dying. Prostitution has been brought out of the ghetto. The world traveller who searches for commercial sex can do so from the comfort of his hotel room. Call girls who leave calling cards are everywhere. Travellers should check the facts first though. In many countries offers of massage are exactly what they seem. A hotel masseur or masseuse in Japan will probably only be interested in your aches and pains.

Another reason that red-light districts are dying is the price of property. People buy cheaply in a run-down area then complain virtuously. Once the girls are out, the price of houses in the area goes up.

I have aimed to cover a representative selection of cities around the world from Europe to the East. Regretfully, I left out Russia and most of Africa and the Middle East. My informants led me to believe that most of the prostitution in Russia was hotel and not red-light district based. Similarly, most of that in Africa seems to be amateur – a hotel employee offers his sister. If she's refused, he offers his brother, and so on. There's the gigolo system too in Gambia. But that does not seem to operate in one district or on a fixed scale of charges – a middle-aged woman just buys herself a black stud in exchange for presents, and a good time is had by all.

Cairo was the furthest I went in Africa. It is one of the sadder pieces in the book. I had considered visiting Tangiers for its gay scene, but friends told me that prostitution is dead there. The beautiful boys are all dying of AIDS. AIDS will certainly end many of the most carelessly run red-light districts. Where sex-workers take endless clients and fail to use condoms the risk is high.

When I started my researches I went in with an open mind. Should prostitution be legal or illegal? I had no fixed idea. After visiting the first few cities I realised that the only hope for the girls (or boys) was legality, or at any rate, decriminalisation of prostitution. When a girl is abused by her client she can expect help from the police, only if her activity is legal. When I interviewed in Ireland, I talked to a girl who showed signs of having taken a most violent beating from one of her regulars. She assured me she could expect no help from the police. I have often thought about her since and feared for her life and safety. In Turkey, by contrast, the prostitution is police run and therefore violence is stopped immediately. In Greece, the police are only a phone call away… Curiously though, while most things to do with sex are legal in Germany, prostitutes claimed that they got little help from the police. They were still certainly better off than Chris in Dublin though.

Another alternative to legalisation is less harassment. This seems to work reasonably well in Brussels and Tel Aviv where the police drive by to keep an eye on things but don't pick anyone up unless there's obvious trouble.

One of the features of the *News of the World*'s stories is that the reporter always leaves when things get serious. That was often the point at which I started interviewing. Mostly I chose to tell the truth about why I was there and let my interviewees know that I was writing a book. It seemed the most honest policy. However, the need for interpreters, or men with local knowledge to help with my story, often meant I had to accommodate myself to their approach. In Los Angeles, Steve, a homeless Jew, introduced me as a Methodist hoping to start a mission in the area. In Hong Kong, my contact took me to his favourite brothel and told the Madame I was running a similar establishment in Hastings and wanted some tips on technique! When I was on my own, I sometimes went to even greater extremes to get my story. In Amsterdam, I became part of a live sex

784648684

act by hanging on to the performer's cock while interviewing him. It was a speedy way of getting introduced and very definitely safe sex. I have never before interviewed anyone in such circumstances and doubt if the opportunity will arise again. I have often wondered what the audience thought of my part in the action. It was winter in Amsterdam and I was very fully dressed in layers of sweaters, thermal underwear and boots. Remarkably, the performer answered lucidly and continued performing while I held on – a true professional, in other words. In Turkey, by contrast, I had to disguise myself as a man to penetrate the brothel area.

As I clocked up more and more red-light districts I found that national characteristics emerged. While I am still convinced that human beings are not bound by the limitations of nationality (or of sex, for that matter) it is fair to say that each red-light district reflected the traits of its country in some way. Some nations prefer straight sex, others are into blowjobs, some take two minutes to come, others take half an hour, and so on…The price of sex also varied out of proportion with the price of other commodities. What could be had for £3 in Izmir might cost £80 in Japan or Mexico. I mentioned this fact to a businessman when, for once in my life, I was travelling first class thanks to an upgrade. He looked like the sort of man who knew the world and its ways. He suggested an ingenious explanation. The comparisons I had made were between the price of a hotel room or a meal and sex. He suggested that there might be one commodity, something underground – a gun or a gram of heroine perhaps – that would bear an exact relation to the price of sex in each country. I'd like to think his strange theory was true, but I haven't tracked down the commodity yet.

While each country produced its stereotypes, the industry, on the whole, didn't. Most of the prostitutes I talked to were intelligent. At the upper end of the market they didn't seem miserable or maladjusted. They had their lives under control. At the lower end many were abused or on drugs, that's true – many, but not all. I felt that their life style was certainly not one to be envied. At the upper end though, if a girl could bear to service unlovely clients, a good living could be had. It's one of very few professions where a person can make enough money to get out and do something else in a short space of time.

My preconceptions about prostitutes were shattered. The same was to happen about my views on the sort of clients that they attract. I had assumed most of them were unattractive, but this is not the case in every country.

When I was dealing with hard facts – the price of sex, the activities engaged in, it was easy to find answers. While the prostitutes seemed to be honest enough in their replies, their clients often revelled in self-deception. About half those who've regaled me with tales of their prostitutional experiences assumed that they were giving the girls wonderful orgasms. While one or two of the prostitutes, Chris of Dublin and Marianna of Mexico, for instance, certainly liked men, I have yet to meet one who has orgasms on a regular basis with her clients. It all goes to prove that most of the profession are rather good actresses… Perhaps, in this day and age, men should assume that women who enjoy having sex with them don't charge for it.

Many of my own false assumptions about the sex industry sprang from reading too many novels. When I got out on the streets to do my research I found out that there are considerably less pimps involved than lurid crime stories would have us believe. I also found that the lavish gentleman's brothel is a thing of the past. Modern-day brothels are generally seedy and utilitarian. I have a French friend who longs to run one in England. She has great style and a flair for fashion – things sadly lacking in the profession's modern exponents, but the rigours of British law prevent her making the experiment…

In dealing with red-light districts I was writing, not merely about prostitution, but about a whole range of related activities, stripping, acting in sex shows, sex shops, etc. The managers of sex-shops around the world were invariably the easiest to interview. Their activity was legal. Usually I interviewed in English, or when forced to it, in bad schoolgirl French. In some countries I did it through the medium of an interpreter. I came across an interesting follow-up to one of my stories when I met a journalist who had interviewed the same sex-shop keeper in Tel Aviv. He had used English; I had done it in Hebrew through a friend. We swapped facts. Both of us were slightly annoyed to discover we'd been given a marginally different story. He had been told that the hottest sellers among videos were those of men shagging horses, while I had got to see the special hermaphroditic sex dolls…

I avoided sociological questions. I wasn't writing that kind of book. My queries were very down to earth and practical. I wasn't interested in proving that every woman on the street has been abused, or that she can't form relationships. I would assume that the truth is something much subtler and varies from individual to individual. Probably the only thing all the professionals I talked to did have in common was a love of money.

One of the problems with writing this book has been funding. Ideally, all the countries should have been visited in a year or so, to make the prices comparable. Funding each visit myself, or working on two projects at once while on press trips, meant that I had to extend the project across several years. I feared at first that prices would soar, making all comparisons irrelevant. However, I soon realised that this was not the case. In a recession, visits to a prostitute are cut back on. Prices keep low. To enable those of my readers who want to do their own research and make their own comparisons I have listed the years in which I visited each city in my list of Acknowledgements.

It was not always easy to find out where exactly to go when I'd chosen my city. In 1993, I spent what should have been a profitable day at the World Travel Market issuing the representatives of some thirty countries with my business card and a request for information. Almost none of the boards came through with what I wanted. Belgium had already given me good information. Zurich followed suit. Germany provided some maps. Yet, almost everywhere else, from Europe to the West Indies, greeted me with sniggers then failed to send anything. A handful of countries took a moralistic tone. South Africa sounded helpful then sent a prim letter saying it was all illegal. China, Russia and the Lebanon took the same tone. My informants in Cairo had all sworn that a certain street in Beirut was stocked with Gulf War widows on the game. It was an interesting story and I would have liked to verify it. But the woman from the Lebanon proved most disapproving of all. The conversation following my initial query ran like this: "No, we have no prostitution in Lebanon!" "Well, can I have a map of Beirut, then?" "No!"

However much tourist boards and the politically correct affirm that such activities don't exist, red-light districts are likely to continue to flourish or fester for many years to come.

# Toronto

TORONTO THE GOOD it's called locally. Peter Ustinov has described it as "New York run by the Swiss". "Canadians prefer ice-hockey to sex," I'd been told. In a city that sells everything you've ever thought of, plus all the things you haven't, there had to be a seamy underside.

Toronto's main sex shop on Yorkville Avenue has an openly Freudian approach. You can buy a nipple cap to put on your beer can, a chocolate penis to melt in your mouth or *The Gentleman's Guide to the Inflated Mistress*. A card above the till carries the immortal line: No exchange or refund on vibrators.

For those who're not into inflatables, there are hookers on Yonge Street at night and boys loitering outside various branches of Macdonald's. Prices are by personal negotiation. Needless to say, the trade is seasonal. A Canadian winter is no time for walking the streets. Other professionals advertise in *Now* magazine. All the men are "hung". "Scottish" is also used liberally as an inducement in the same way we'd use "Swedish".

Yonge Street's a paradise for fetishists. From Dundas Street northwards the strip clubs start. The clothes stock everything from Chinese silk-satin lingerie, leather and Shanghai-made Irish crochet see-through blouses to cerise Lycra jock straps in *Muscle Mag's Muscle Shoppe*, or chain mail and corsets in *Blitz Mode*.

Table dancing is Canada's sex speciality. Quebec girls are rumoured to be best. Stripping used to feature alongside burlesque – something that has died out almost everywhere, with the exception of local legend Liz Lyons. She still performs in her eighties, although for the last ten years she has kept her clothes on.

Girls in the taverns carry stools on their heads and can be asked to dance on them for five dollars minimum. Some young designers use this as a chance to show off beach wear, lingerie, stretch microskirts or leather, while earning enough in tips to finance their business. Their earnings can be good – 1,600 to 2,500 dollars a week for the best ones.

Strip joints have become more respectable since the Mafia moved out to the suburbs. There was a mammoth clean up in the Seventies after a shoeshine boy was raped then drowned in a sink by two men. The government funds some of the clubs now. Policemen descend occasionally, stay for five minutes, watch a little of the show, then leave.

I sampled both male and female strip-clubs in the company of Bruce Meyer, poet and academic. He had been unwise enough to offer me a tour of the town, so I cajoled him into believing these were the only things I hadn't seen.

We started at the *Zanzibar*. One girl performs the floorshow at a time. Her props are a fireman's pole and a shower cabinet. Part of the act involves whirling round the pole at speed. The act extends across three songs. On the last song the knickers come off.

In *Chippendale's* the acts involve the audience. Male strippers sit on your lap or take you on to the stage. The amount they show is up to the individuals. The first dancer was coy and kept shifting a little white towel in front of his genitals like a toreador with the bull. Some of the dancers simulate masturbation.

The difference between the two bars was marked. In the first, men were drinking and talking to each other, hardly sparing a glance for the girl performers. In the second, all the women (and one gay man) were intent. The second dancer, *The Outlaw*, (definitely "hung"), offered to do a table dance for me, after his act. Bruce kept his back demurely turned while the Outlaw took me off into the corner and got me to sit at a low table with my knees tucked under. He stood on the table and began to dance. Turning his back towards me, he stretched out his hands for mine and ran them over his body. Seemingly the no-touch rule Bruce had told me about wasn't enforced everywhere.

A table-dance is much more erotic than a floorshow, because it's done personally for you and the genitals are on eye-level. Still, having a streak of the mean Scot in me, I was determined to get more for my five dollars and interviewed The Outlaw. By day he was a law student. His dancing financed the course. He was Greek with an Italian fiancée whom he remained faithful to. He had danced in America for years. Unfortunately, he couldn't make his act as funny in Toronto – Canadians weren't amused when he put his head up ladies' skirts and kissed their thighs, he complained. By now, Bruce was champing to leave, and muttered something about feeling like Virgil, showing me round the underworld.

Canada is a huge country and other cities do not follow the same pattern as Toronto. For one thing, most of them are not quite as cosmopolitan. I have not visited other major cities in Canada, but

my hairdresser swears that the scene in Montreal is tied into burlesque and the black cabaret tradition. In Calgary, I was told by a
holidaymaker, hookers solicit outside churches, hoping to get the
congregation as they come out all fired up with love. In Victoria,
dire occult things are supposed to go on... I wrote to find out about
the latter and prostitution in various other cities, but the tourist
board told me that all such things were illegal and did not go on...

# Amsterdam

AMSTERDAM'S RED-LIGHT district probably gets through more kitchen-rolls in a night than most countries use in a week. In the early morning, you can see vanloads being delivered to theatres and cinemas in the area. And that's not counting the private supplies used by the girls. Through every window into a small bedroom, you can see one of these rolls lying on a bed. The rooms used for prostitution are cramped and unattractive. Most of the women are dressed in underwear only – a Basque or teddy, G-string or pants, bare legs or stockings and suspenders. A lot are overweight and rather plain. The only good-looking women in the business seem to be Asian ones. Some of the girls only charge 35 guilders (about £12). It must take a great many tricks to get rich, or even stay solvent, once the rent of the cubicle's deducted. Most of the men in the street are just passers-by. When one lingers, the girl he's watching starts to feel herself, running her hands over her pants or pulling her tits out of her Basque, even if he already has a girl with him. Prostitutes make the assumption that couples might be hoping to watch each other on the job with her, or might want a threesome. Some of the roads have had prostitutes on the same spot for centuries, since the days when Amsterdam was a more important port than Rotterdam. There's little business done on the street these days though – not prostitution, anyway.

Recently, the area has become more violent, with the odd mugging – mainly by junkies after the price of the next fix. The down side of the Wallen or Quays is that there are pushers galore on the street. I didn't actually see any myself but I was told by a man who'd lived there with a rich heroin addict, that they just wouldn't allow her to give up – someone was always offering her a free packet, every time she walked down the road. However much the pimps try to police the streets to keep them attractive for tourists, crime rears its ugly head. In many cases it's the tourists misbehaving, of course. English drunks can't resist the chance to throw each other into the canal in the early hours.

Apart from throwing each other into canals, the other thing you must not do is take photographs. The red-light district's a place of permanent Saturnalia where people go to lead the other half of their double lives in a sort of public privacy. Homosexuals come from

England to be able to hold hands and show tenderness on the street like any other couple, transvestites and leatherboys to show off or get clients. The prostitutes in the windows may have another, respectable family life in another district, or be sending money home to parents in Indonesia, pretending that they work in a bar. If you want to use your camera to record anything you must pay. Everything has its price.

On the plus side, the area is full of interest. A good many of the houses around the *Wallen* are two to three centuries old and beautifully proportioned inside. This and the multinational Bohemian atmosphere attract a lot of artists and writers. There are also pubs, bars and cafés with seemingly stronger coffee than elsewhere and good Indonesian and Chinese food.

The main roads lead to other districts of Amsterdam, so men in them may simply be passing through. There's one alleyway, though, that terminates in a brothel of sorts. Men who walk up that street mean business. The architecture's more like a run-down concrete shopping centre than the sort of sumptuous bordello you see in films. It's not visually interesting – just a collection of half a dozen or so girls in windows. Curiously, it was built by two artists.

Just round the corner I came on the *Condomerie* – an honestly named shop that sells every shape and flavour that the most devious mind could devise. I only gave the most cursory glance at the more general sex shops. In common with that in British sex shops, the underwear on show in Amsterdam ones lacks sensuous eroticism. The minuscule G-strings and peephole bras were all glaringly bright colours of nylon, with or without marabou. There was not a vestige of silk in sight. The range of vibrators and so on also seemed similar – when you've seen one phosphorescent French tickler, you've seen them all. Perhaps there were more (and larger) dildoes on display than elsewhere, but perhaps that was my fancy. The only major difference is that some shops advertise that they know all the laws on getting videos through customs. Amsterdam is renowned for having hard porn videos that you can't buy in England or many other countries.

Separate establishments offer peepshows. For two and a half guilders (about 80p) I was able to look at a couple making love under bright light on a circular revolving bed surrounded by windows for other onlookers. You put the money in a slot and a blind rises, allowing you to look in. I found myself staring instead at the

Arab guy at the opposite window. Down on the bed, what was going on might well have been simulation rather than penetration. The girl was pretty, but the man was rather flabby with flea bites and stretch marks on his bum. I was decidedly bored by the end of my two minutes or so, and could hardly wait for the shutter to come down automatically.

Live sex shows are probably what Amsterdam's red-light district is most famed for in England. Ours went years ago. Even when they were there, from what I've heard, they were of little more interest than the peepshow. I saw my first live sex show at the *Theatre Casa Rosa* beside the *Oude Zijts* canal. The doorman, a young student earning a little extra at nights, was touting for custom in various languages, but mostly English. He even changed his accent periodically to lure Americans. He told them about "the lovely girls", changing it back to "family show" to attract the British. About the only "family" thing about it was the fact that one of the live sex acts happened to be a married couple having their conjugal rights in every conceivable position (barring the missionary one) in public and for money. It must be a nice way to earn your living if you're exhibitionistically inclined.

Performers are paid from 225 guilders for a stripper to 350 a night for the male half of a sex act (£75 to £120). The higher pay for men is not so much sexism as a reasonable belief that sustaining an erection is worth better wages than just lying back and thinking of Holland. Married couples are paid their fee together – so it's up to them how they split it.

Some years ago the theatres and houses on this bank were torched by an arsonist. Performers, tarts and clients were seen leaping from windows in various costumes, or none at all – a sight that would have been funny if thirteen people hadn't lost their lives.

While I was scanning the photos outside the theatre, an old man, with a handlebar moustache curled up in nets, sidled up to me and said, "For eleven years I am champion of the Nederlands!" He handed me his card:
Ome Joop
11 iaar *Mister Snor*
(Moustache)
*van Nederland*
*nu Mister International*
There was a photo of him on it with his moustaches unfurled to

all their glorious length. Quite why he was standing outside a sex show handing out his business card I will probably never know. Perhaps he was touting for some very unusual kind of work..

I was allowed in free at the *Theatre Casa Rosa* because I was with a writer who lived in the area. The proprietors didn't wish to charge a neighbour, they said. Our first Heineken came free also. It was early and there were few in the audience. Men exited at intervals. Being naturally bad-minded, I assumed it was for a wank until I saw most of them later, lounging by the bar upstairs.

A live sex show consists of a number of acts, some solo, others in pairs, and so on. Whenever it was needed, an oval bed rose majestically on stage. A section of the stage was able to revolve with the bed, giving other views. The acts go on in rotation from 8.30 at night till three in the morning. The males in the sex acts have the difficult task of being erect, smiling and able to perform about seven times a night.

All the acts in the show are choreographed professionally. Talent scouts poach likely performers from other theatres, persuading them they'd look great in a gorilla-suit and dildo, or whatever. Of course, a gorilla-suit is a great cover if you happen to see your neighbour in the front row...

The show was surprisingly entertaining, but more comic than erotic. It had many of the qualities of old music hall or burlesque. As a turn-on it failed for me. I felt a certain arousal at the beginning of the sex acts but that faded soon. I could feel much more desire from spending an hour or two talking to any attractive man. Perhaps the music was too loud. Perhaps it was all too comic to take seriously. At one point I laughed till I almost cried as *Rudolph the Red-nosed Reindeer* came over the loudspeakers while the dark pink Lurex curtains closed between acts. As it was late December, it was a dead cert that Father Christmas would get involved sooner or later – he did.

For looks and flexibility, the long languorous blonde stripper who started the show won hands down. The most enjoyable act for me was Batman rescuing "Sammy Jo" (tied to a pole in an artistically torn dress) then being sucked off as he walked round the revolving bed, his mammoth cock still in her mouth, before going on to have sex with her. I also liked the man in a gorilla suit accompanying a black girl in a red wig, carrying maracas. They were obviously enjoying themselves and the fun spilt over into the audience as they tried to get people to participate.

The gorilla fondled my tits in passing as he went up the aisle, then stuck his brown plastic prick in an Englishman's ear in the front row. It was all good (if not clean) fun – in any case, nobody likes to argue with a gorilla. The Englishman's wife soothed her husband out of his state of shock by patting his head and muttering something (probably, "There, there!") The first time round, the girl with the maracas, accompanied by Carmen Miranda music, called for five strong men to help in her act. She was on a loser – there weren't five-strong men in the audience and the weak ones were busy trying not to be seen, sliding down lower in their seats to avoid being picked. I thought I might be the next best thing to a strong man – I've been told I've got balls – so I volunteered, hoping to get the ball rolling, as it were, and took a bite of about a quarter of an inch off the banana she'd placed between her legs. I figured what was coming and knew the first bite would be safe. The rest of the strong men slunk off to the bar and the act fell flat. "You've spoiled her banana!" my companion said. Next time round, she was in luck. There was a stag party in the front row. Five men volunteered at once. The last of them was dressed as Father Christmas. As he took the final bite a pair of black legs locked nimbly round his neck and held him while he struggled feebly to get away.

Most of those in the audience were tourists. Probably the only time Dutch people go to the Casa Rosa is for a stag party. There were a couple of those in, the night I was there. Some of the men, like Father Christmas, were in fancy dress. Another man had come dressed as a Sheikh with a false nose and a bib round his neck, saying, "*Ik ben de baas*" (I am the boss.)

Not all the tourists were amused. I don't know whether it was the gorilla squirting his dildo on stage, or Father Christmas meeting his fate, but it was all too much for a young Japanese girl who forced the men who'd brought her in to take her out again almost as soon as they'd arrived. They didn't even get to sit down. Three other women also left when the semi-naked black girl lay on the laps of the men in front. I had little sympathy with them. Whatever the tout was saying about a "family show", the pictures outside were explicit enough to let them know exactly what they were getting into.

Batman came by again. I've always been mesmerised by men who offer to lead me up on stage. The last time it happened I was ten – a conjuror gave me his wand and it turned floppy in my hand. This time the rod in my hand did not wilt. Seeing things that close, I can certainly vouch for the penetration not being faked. Remembering my journalistic duty, even at a time like that, I attempted to interview the poor man while he was bonking away and I was holding one of Sammy Jo's legs (as requested). I figured a sex-performer could cope with holding a polite conversation at a time like that. It must have been a funny sight for the audience as I half reclined, fully-dressed against the cold: two sweaters, long skirt, leather belt, silk knickers, tights and clumping shoes – thoroughly proof against even the most determined rapist. The most poor Batman could manage in five minutes was a hand up my skirt. Lying beside a bored, silent Sammy Jo, I kept trying to ask him everyday questions about his work, while playing Robin to his Batman. I didn't do too well – he was more interested in getting me to join in more thoroughly. Besides, the management didn't like performers giving interviews, I was told. I was offered a suck or a fuck, but I pointed out there was no chance as I wasn't getting paid for it. In despair, perhaps assuming I was a dyke, as I'd come there with a woman, he offered me Sammy Jo. Did I want to fondle her tits? He asked – I could if I liked. No, I haven't done anything like that since I was fourteen and at a single sex school. I might well turn lesbian if I ever get incarcerated in a woman's prison – but until that day, I'd much rather fondle other things, thank you very much.

Only one of the acts made me feel slightly uneasy. The music changed to *Smoke Gets in Your Eyes* as she stripped, lit a fat cigar and went into a shoulder-stand, puffing away at it through her fanny. You couldn't help watching, as the glowing end moved around, seemingly dangerously near her bare thighs. Smoke was getting absolutely everywhere but in her eyes. Most performers lie about their jobs to family and friends – I found myself wondering just how she explained the presence of tar and nicotine when she went for her cervical smear tests.

The cast is multi-national – Australian, Yugoslavian, African, Indonesian, Dutch. Weren't there any English? I asked. Yes – the two lesbians – but they were off for the night. (Curiously, when we asked the theatre nearby if they had a lesbian act, they said they weren't going to have one tonight because the Theatre Casa Rosa wasn't doing one. Perhaps all the lesbians were off having a hen party together.) It was a pity – I would rather have liked to see a lesbian act, to see how it was staged. Anaïs Nin, in Kaufman's film, *Henry And June*, makes the point that such acts always show one woman aping a male role, where, in reality, lesbian sex is only rarely about that. If this tradition is maintained in Amsterdam, the scene would probably be performed with a dildo and one woman on top. Perhaps it's unreasonable to expect anything else. Could anyone be tender in five minutes and in public?

Even if acts don't have to be tender, males certainly have to be erect. Just how do performers manage it on cue? I asked one of them if they sustained it by fantasy. Not at all. "I know I have to – it's my job. Without that I don't earn." It was as simple as that. Of course, the girl sucking him to start with might have helped. Apart from the standard wage, there could be opportunities, too, for a bit of freelance, on-the-side prostitution. I heard a story of a male performer being given 1,000 guilders for a night with an Australian actress who liked the look of what he had.

If performers fancy each other, on the other hand, it can sometimes create problems. It could be hard to leave off at the end of your turn. You might also ejaculate on stage. The night I was there nobody came, apart from the gorilla. On the rare occasions when someone does, it's thought best to make it obvious by coming on the face or breasts of a partner.

Occasionally, nasty scenes erupt if drunken honeymooners (usually English) get involved with the sex acts. The husband might like the idea of seeing his wife up there with a stud, but reproach her and quarrel afterwards. There can be jealousy, too, if one of the performers has a boyfriend or girlfriend who doesn't work on the sex scene. One girl's live-in boyfriend was turning up night after night to torture himself in the front row. "Why don't you go in an act yourself?" her fellow-performers asked him. But no, he believed (in common with about half the male population) that his genitals weren't big enough to be seen in public!

The people who perform are as varied as in any other profession. Some seem to be enjoying their work; others look bored. It's certainly a better life, though, than sitting in a window, kitchen-roll at the ready. What all the performers have in common is a desire to make some money to finance their dreams – whether it is going into business for themselves, or something odder. One of the girls, I was told, had the strange hobby of collecting Barbie dolls. She had six hundred of them, filling a room at home.

# Amsterdam II: Hanky Panky's Tattoo Parlour

HANKY PANKY'S TATTOO PARLOUR along the *Oude Zijts Voorburgwal* in Amsterdam contains one of the most unusual museums you could wish to find. It's one of those quirky, idiosyncratic collections run by one man – a monument to the bizarre. Henk Schiffmacher, himself a practising tattooist, has brought together what is probably the world's most comprehensive collection of designs, tools and pictures, related to his art. Yet, all the major guidebooks choose to ignore it. Henk still tattoos there. You can make an appointment and choose what you want to have done.

Tattooing is taken very seriously in Amsterdam. Tattooists even have their own union with sixty-five members. It is very important, since AIDS, that the profession is carefully regulated. Every customer has his own needle.

Once inside you're confronted with a notice: "Children must be kept quiet and strictly under control while they are in this shop." It wouldn't be an easy task with the variety of objects on display. The first case in the centre contains several decades' worth of tools, all carefully labelled with their donors' names. To the left and the right are other cases full of the old pattern books of designs, complete with sailors' greasy thumb-prints, plus other items like an Indian tattooist's travel-kit with jars of powdered colours and a Delft plate from the Amsterdam Tattooists' Convention back in 1934. Unexplained oddities – like a stuffed monkey in one of the cabinets – lend colour. The pattern books, particularly the older ones, have some artistic merit. It's interesting to see the changing shape of the women men want tattooed on their arms or chest – old images mirrored the films of the day closely. There are Gibson girls and Rita Hayworth clones by the score. More exotic all-over designs from New Zealand, the Philippines and many other places are also represented – colourful dragons interwoven with mythological figures. Tattooing from the most primitive pop or comic cut western designs to the complicated beautiful oriental pictures, is essentially fantasy art.

Most interesting to me was the large collection of photos of satisfied customers and those with interesting or unusual tattoos displayed around the walls. The quality of the pictures is good.

The majority of the subjects are male. Again a variety of national designs is represented, including tribal scarification. I found the European photographs more interesting. I enjoyed reading the psychology of the sitters by their obvious expressions of pride, prurience, aggression or embarrassment. Amusingly, there was one of a naked couple on a very bourgeois ribbed Dralon couch. The husband had managed by careful positioning of a raised knee, to hide his wife's genitals and breasts while displaying all his and her tattoos.

Some tattoos are more artistic than others. I liked best a purely surrealistic photo of someone bending forward with a highly realistic man's face on his bald pate.

Although naked ladies are a common subject, erotic tattoos of lovers are a rarity. There was only one example on display. The man was immortalised in the act of penetration, still wearing his open-necked shirt, while his woman (in high heels) reclined on a red cushion.

The museum is the perfect place for a ghoul's day out. Definitely not for the squeamish is the cast of a tattooed Maori head with what looks like real teeth and hair implanted. Even more stomach-turning are the pictures of infibulation. Was that murky photo of a thing that looked like a Chinese gooseberry pierced with a series of seven steel rings what I thought? Yes, it was. More artistically, another example was tattooed like an owl fetish with wings rising above. Rings through the tip were connected by chains to a chastity belt. On the thighs, a donkey and leopard looked across in horror at what lay between. Curiously, none of the pictures of infibulation included the proud owners' faces. Not so coy are those who've merely had their members tattooed. I liked best the picture of a squint-eyed sailor proudly displaying an octopus on his shaved pubic area, one tentacle of which wound its way round and round and down and down. Even women have been known to have this kind of tattoo. One photo shows an Asian girl with a devil's face on her pubic bone, half-obscured by her unshaven hair.

Perhaps even more disturbing than the "Chinese gooseberry" or the owl with chains was the preserved foetus complete with its umbilical chord. A tiny blue heart had been tattooed on the left of its chest. I'd like to have known the story behind that. Was it a bizarre commission from a grief-stricken parent, or a horrible joke using leftover remains saved from the hospital incinerator?

# Tokyo and Kyoto

I HAD BEEN warned before I went to Kyoto that the strip shows were a little different there. Since Japanese censors started blacking out a certain area on the models in sex mags, Man's natural curiosity about that area grew. You can see the front row of respectable businessmen turning their heads with more than Western interest to examine the cunts of the girls. After every strip routine, the girls return with a Polaroid camera and spread their legs so that members of the audience can take close-up photos for tips of 500 Yen (about £2). Just what the wives of the respectable businessmen think when they press their husbands' suits and come on the Polaroid in the pocket, is another matter...

Japanese men are refreshingly up front and open about owning up to a kink for porn. I'm told some even quote it as a hobby when they are on TV game shows.

Kyoto's chief strip show is held nightly in the *DX Tohji de Luxe*. It's so popular that most of the similar theatres in other cities in Japan are called after it. *The Tohji* is actually the name of the Buddhist temple next door. *Ji* in compound words means a temple. The monks, of course, never venture to see the show next door. "It's a gay world in Buddhist temples," the manager of my hotel assured me. What DX stands for no one – Japanese or Western – has been able to tell me. Perhaps it's equivalent to our X-rated, because it turns up in the names of other theatres. The Tohji used to host a very different kind of entertainment. The manager of the hotel I was staying at was an ex-habitué and swore that it was "a fucking show". Funny, as I remember it, fucking takes two. All the girls I saw were solo acts doing a very slow strip routine, starting with extremely romantic clothes like a white lace crinoline and parasol or black leather, fishnet and all the works. There were also a good few feather boas. When performers returned to the stage for pictures after their acts they wore something simple – a jersey mini dress with leopard spots, a ra-ra skirt or a wrap-over version of a French maid's skirt trimmed in marabou. The girls are pretty but westernised Japanese – mostly taller than average with long legs and hennaed crimped hair.

The audience on that night was remarkably noisy. I was told that it was students in there at the weekend – fans of the girls – but they looked like plants to me. Several men and women of twenty or so were thumping tambourines, screaming, blowing whistles and pumping up long phallic balloons which floated away to the mirrored ceiling or popped on the hot lights above the two circular stages below. There was a slightly repulsive fake jollity about the whole thing.

I heard lots were drawn for the girls and the lucky winners had it off on stage at one time – but not the night I was there. These days it's down to the odd discreet bargain by the stage door.

Closedown happened at a surprisingly early time – 10.45. There are odd bars open in Kyoto in the small hours, but most of the city seems to go to bed surprisingly early. It's remarkably hard to find any vice in Kyoto. I had been told there was a street for prostitutes behind my hotel – and near another temple – but on my way back from the show, I was the only woman on it.

Perhaps the rise of blue movies and videos has put paid to a lot of the stronger sex shows. One of our party swore that he saw a titillating snatch of female Sumo wrestlers falling on each other in the early hours on the pay channel of his hotel TV – it was getting really interesting, he said, when his 100 yen coins ran out.

You need to go to Tokyo these days, if you fancy a stronger show than those in Kyoto. Tokyo, under its earlier name, Edo, was known as "the city of pleasure" According to James Kirkup's *Gaijin On The Ginza*, there are Apollo Bars for lesbians, a great many pick-up points for homosexuals, not to mention the chance of a good feel in the crowded tube trains. The best coaches for this, he states, are the last, second to last and first. But I was never travelling in the rush hour to test his theory. I did ask about the Apollo Bars, though – but nobody had heard of them.

The red-light district of Tokyo is known euphemistically as "an entertainment area". *Kabuki-cho* is on the east of Shinjuku station. You enter it by a red arch. Interestingly, it is on the site of the old *Yoshiwara* area famous for its geishas. Geishas still exist, but I'm told that they are mostly sixty or seventy and so hold little appeal for young men.

The area abounds in Love Hotels. The average rate is 6000 Yen an hour (£24), although there are cheaper ones. If they're labelled in English, look for names such as *Hotel Venus* or *Hotel Me And You*. Their users could be a married couple trying to get a little peace away from their small Japanese home with paper-thin walls, young people who still live at home and are also after privacy, or prostitutes and their clients. I haven't tried one out myself, but I'm told they have washing facilities, blue movies, condoms and sometimes extras like vibrators or dildoes. Altogether they sound like rather a good idea – a way of keeping people off the streets. When a Japanese man asked me why we didn't have an equivalent in Britain, I told him we use our cars. Come to think of it, that may well be why British cars look in considerably worse condition than Japanese ones.

The funniest story I came across about Love Hotels was that of an employee of Japan Airlines. He had been called to Tokyo for a sudden meeting and found there wasn't a room to be had anywhere except in the Love Hotels. The clerk at the desk raised an eyebrow when he checked in alone. He was even more surprised when he came back an hour later to beg for a piece of string. (In case you're wondering – he only intended to wash his smalls and hang them up to dry.) I expect the tale has gone down as a proof of British kinkiness with the Japanese.

For a *gaijin* (foreigner), it's a little difficult to find anything in Japan. Although it's simple enough to learn some elementary phrases of spoken Japanese, the written form is a different matter. The language runs to three separate alphabets: *hiragana* for truly Japanese words, *katakana* for foreign words transcribed and *kanji* – Chinese characters which represent a word or a syllable. It's the kanji that create the greatest problem. There are several thousand to be learned – a great many Japanese haven't mastered more than the simplest few hundred. Then there's the address system. Many road names aren't even written up in *kanji*, let alone English. The numbering also has a system entirely its own. You often won't find a logical pattern down a road. It's usually done on a first come first served basis. Early builders start at number one. As houses or shops are added they get a higher number. If they built from left to right or right to left, it could work – but when shops are fitted in between shops, that's a different matter.

While the side streets full of Love Hotels are obvious, it could take you some time to track down other things. In my search for strip clubs I mounted various stairs only to be confronted by Karaoke clubs or perfectly harmless pubs and restaurants, of which Kabuki-cho has a good many. In desperation I tried any bar with a slightly dubious sounding name in English characters. But alas,

*Adult Snacks* just turned out to be a café and not a bar with illicit, displays of oral sex as my bad mind had suspected. The first night I was there, I started looking too late and found a couple of doormen passed out on the floor of two different clubs, snoring blissfully. While Kyoto closes down at 10.45, Tokyo's all done by 12 – there's a police rule about that.

You will come across video shops, massage parlours and an abundance of gambling dens, but the live shows are harder to find. For those you need the help of a tout, some of whom speak little English. If you're male, they will probably hassle you whether you're interested or not. Unfortunately, most of them will try to direct you to Karaoke bars where there are beautiful girls – or so they say. I got my entrée to one of the illegal strip clubs by asking an artist who was selling paintings by the side of the road. He looked Mediterranean so I figured that he might speak a language I was more proficient in than Japanese. He referred me to a tout who had a few English phrases, and soon we were ushered into the *DX Kabuki-cho*, where a show was already in progress.

The audience was mostly Japanese with the odd Korean or Filipino, apart from a horribly attentive Iranian who kept turning his head on one side and looking up the girls' cunts with the most aesthetic expression on his face. The music was disco hits, sometimes English ones, with an usher bashing a tambourine. As with a lot of Japanese piped music, bird-song is sometimes edited on to the track.

The noise factor in the *DX Kabuki-cho* was more tolerable than that in Kyoto. There was a Lurex backdrop and a revolving mirror-covered ball hit by a spotlight. Before some acts, smoke from dry ice poured on to the stage.

Towards the end of each go-go routine, the girls would strike a number of poses that showed their genital area clearly. Often, when they bent forward legs apart in high heels, they'd part the labia with their fingers. Whenever a clitoris was revealed the audience clapped loudly.

The girls were mostly of an extremely high level of looks. Some were positively beautiful. The female magician, though, was more ordinary – but then she had other talents…

Before each girl came on, an announcement was made: *Hostessu Iasko… Hostessu Uno… Hostessu Mitsu…* etc. The first stripper was already retreating and another came on briefly in a shocking-pink sequin evening dress and huge hat worthy of Danny La Rue. Next came the female magician. I christened her Paula Daniels.

After the initial strip routine where she got down to a tiny orange leather microskirt with a Smurf-sized plastic Buddha hanging from a button at the waist, "Paula Daniels" pulled several metres of flimsy scarf out of her cunt. With a little help from the men in the front row she extracted a further length of pink ribbon and a yellow Ping-Pong ball. Then she took a large paint brush of the kind used for calligraphy out of the little plastic peg-basket that most Japanese strippers carry on with their Polaroid cameras at the end. She dipped her brush in a china pot of ink and inserted it into her cunt. Squatting with her legs wide apart above a square of card on the stage floor she drew a complicated *kanji* character in the best calligraphic style. The audience clapped enthusiastically. Then she approached the front row again, joking with the men. She asked one of them for a cigarette. He lit it and, inevitably, she was into a shoulder-stand smoking it down almost to the last puff through her cunt. She put the last half-inch back into the donor's mouth and he finished it.

Next, she brought an egg out of her box and inserted it with a little help from her fans as she kept up her patter to the front row. It turned out to be a fresh egg – she cracked it into a little metal pan with a long handle similar to those found by the wells outside Buddhist temples and used for purification. Her eager victim drank up his egg, smacking his lips. Raw or extremely lightly cooked eggs sometimes feature in Japanese breakfasts, so it was more palatable to him than it would have been to a Westerner. After the egg routine, two men let off firecrackers on the end of a string that disappeared up between her legs.

I am told that Japan has no equivalent to the RSPCA, which is probably why Paula Daniels could get away with inserting a live goldfish, fresh from the bowl, up her cunt. She paraded around the audience inviting men to pull at a tiny bit of protruding tail. One tried, but it stayed fast. Eventually she went back to the centre of the stage, squatted over the bowl and two goldfish plopped into it. She carried it off stage, coming back for applause and to wipe the water splash up with an orange lace handkerchief. Now, either the second goldfish had been lurking up there for the last few minutes, or she'd used the old conjuror's ruse of hiding a thin sliver of fish-shaped carrot about her person. The first fish, though, I'm sure was real. If it had come out stunned, I suppose she could always have sliced it up for sushi.

The next girl came on in a white PVC sailor suit, doing semaphore with a set of flags. She had bobbed hair and looked rather sweet and innocent until she got down to her tiny skirt and red sequinned leg warmers and wrist bands hooked to her middle fingers. There was a mark by her groin, covered with Elastoplast, which got the men next to me speculating. She went off briefly, returning in bunny ears and a pink satin French maid's skirt trimmed with marabou. Soon she was passed from man to man in the front row. She lay in their laps, allowing them to wank her and feel her nipples. She was smiling and laughing as they prodded her clumsily – some of them looked sadly inexperienced – but at the same time she looked unhappy. I have a little book given me by Japan Airlines, *Simple Etiquette In Japan*, which explains the Japanese habit of turning up the corners of the mouth while speaking. Apparently, creases at the corners of the eyes show real happiness. "Paula" had been crinkling, but the sailor-girl was not as she rubbed the hands of strangers on her cunt. She gave one a handkerchief that had been pressed against her and issued tissues from her box to the rest of the front row. Halfway round the row, she found a man who would not put his hands on her cunt. She took his glasses and rubbed them in herself, taking them across to another man who inserted the shafts into her. Then the glasses went back to their owner – they were steamed up, to put it mildly. He exited hurriedly. Out came the Polaroid camera again. An American had his photo taken with her on his lap, with one of her legs held up like a ballet dancer's. Then a young Japanese man was photographed with her. He gripped her breasts frantically as if they were the only pair he'd ever got his hands on.

The next act came on in what was almost a bride's dress, long white and romantic with silver high heels beneath and a huge black garden party hat. She took a long time to strip down to suspenders and black stockings. When she came back, she was trailing a silver negligee. A man from the audience gave her his can of beer.

After her, the next act had a slightly more Japanese flavour. She was wearing a red happi coat embroidered with birds and a gold sash. She did a simple short strip routine.

The next girl made a decidedly Western start. She danced vigorously in silver Lurex hot pants with a matching belt, a black PVC bra and a gold lamé PVC jacket with studded collar. She wore enormous diamanté earrings. Her hair was pulled back into a ponytail. Sensibly, unlike some of the other dancers, she wore flat jazz boots for her routine. Hers were jewelled with large red rhinestones. Before her poses she unlaced her shoes and put on high heels, stripping down to an elegant black diamanté-studded G-string. The music changed as she went off. Thunder sounded and lightning strobed the stage. *Miserere* came across the loudspeakers. She returned in a circular two-tone orange and apricot pleated dress that she spread out like a butterfly as she danced. The dress dropped to the floor at the end of her dance. Unlike the other dancers she had shaved her pubic hair. She advanced on all fours across the stage then held various contorted poses. The men in the front row were fascinated as she parted the lips. They could see a tiny bit of something up there. What was it? A flesh-pink counter holding her lips apart? It was a case of "now you see it, now you don't". Parts of the words of the song were audible: "You can't take away my dignity." (Oh, no?) and something about "love of all inside of me". The men were all turning their heads on one side with the same aesthetic expression as the Iranian, or wiping the sweat from their brows. At last, after five minutes' dancing and suspense, the truth was revealed. Out popped a medium-sized vibrator that had remained inside during her last routine. The audience cheered and catcalled uproariously. For them, this was undoubtedly the best act of the night.

A girl in a silver lamé frock coat came on next. She had large bruises on her bum. Some of the men in the audience touched her. She wrapped her legs round the neck of one of them and he sucked her. The man in the middle was seriously into cunnilingus, because he'd had a little with one or two of the other girls. Streamers descended from above, some of which caught between the girl's legs and men took these and pocketed them for souvenirs.

The last girl was draped in white gauze hanging from her hat. Her bra and hat were both covered with silk pink and white flowers. She wore a white parachute silk sarong skirt, parting to show loose ruched white satin leggings over violet suede boots. She used a chair as a prop. It was also draped in white gauze. She took the hat off to dance, but put it on again before stripping, ending up rolling in the white gauze, fingering herself through it while the speakers played not music any longer, but the sound of sea birds. She returned to the stage with her camera, in a purple mini-dress and white satin gloves under brilliant violet light.

It was the last act, and the audience was played out to the strains of *Auld Lang Syne*. They had played it too in Kyoto. Obviously it's a recognised ending there as much as the National Anthem used to be in Britain.

My companions had defected an act or two earlier in search of a beer. The theatre had no bar – a pity, it could have done a roaring trade. Some of the men in the audience had brought their own drinks. A lot were on the unappealingly named local energy drink – Pocari Sweat. Left to my own devices I naturally got talking to the men in the audience. It was then that I met Koji. He was on holiday from Woking, which meant that he had perfect English.

By one of those curious coincidences that always seem to happen when you're far from home, I soon found out that he had once lived a few houses away from where I spent my youth in Ealing Common. I told Koji that I was a journalist. He had assumed that already from the fact that I was taking notes – something not ordinarily seen in strip shows. He offered to give me the insider tour of Kabuki-cho. We passed Paula Daniels on the street, making her way home in a prim little red suit.

The show we had seen was illegal, I was told. Ordinary stripping was allowable but this had gone further. A little advert in the *Tokyo City Guide* had told punters where to go and offered a thousand-yen discount, getting them in for 3000 Yen (£12) instead of 4000 Yen (£16). The shows keep one step ahead of the police by moving premises every ten days or so.

What did the girls earn? I asked. Koji said that he'd worked out that it was about £500 a night. I thought that unlikely, though, as the theatre only held a hundred or so and was unlikely to sell more than two hundred tickets even allowing for some standing in the aisles and coming and going amongst the squeamish, or those in search of refreshments. Perhaps his reckoning was over-optimistic or assumed a little prostitution on the side.

I told Koji I would like to see a typical sex shop – all in the cause of research. I'd passed a shop labelled *Porn And Video Boutique* but it had only contained films. We soon came to Tokyo's sex shop, but alas, it was closed for refurbishment. At least I assume that's why there were planks lying around in the window.

Next we went to look at some working girls in operation. The street prostitutes, Koji explained, were almost all Korean or Filipino immigrants. On our way we passed a mass of dilapidated shed-like constructions. These were illegal pubs I was told. They had been botched together during the last war out of whatever scrap wood was handy. They had stayed, thanks to backhanders to the authorities. As they fell apart they were patched with more pieces of plywood or odd timbers. Some of them looked little bigger than chicken-houses, with narrow alleys between them.

There were a lot of men on the streets now. Some of them were young, slight and pretty, so I assumed they were male prostitutes. But I was wrong. They turned out to be touts from whom Koji obtained information. Others more sinister-looking, he defined as Mafia or gangsters. From the ordinary man or woman's point of view, though, it has to be said that Tokyo is one of the world's safest cities to walk round in. Mugging or even cheating you in shops don't seem to be part of the Japanese character.

There were stands of porn magazines outside some shops now although most were closed as it was after 12. All the phone boxes were plastered with multi-coloured call girl's cards. There were so many packed on each box that they looked like Victorian screens covered with scraps. Virtually all the cards were in Japanese characters only.

The main prostitution street was ill lit, unlike the rest of Kabuki-cho, which is alive with neon signs. Koji had the bright idea of talking to one of the girls in English in front of me so that I could hear the rates. He walked ahead a little and two girls came up to him. He pretended to be Korean and unable to speak much Japanese, asking her to use English instead. One of the girls knew some English and told him that her charge was 20,000 Yen and 6,000 for the room – presumably a Love Hotel. According to a newspaper article I read later this is the standard going rate. Eighty pounds is a great deal higher than street prostitutes would charge in most cities for basic sex – but then, wages and the cost of living are both high in Japan. I asked the name of the street, once Koji refused the girl. There was nothing to indicate it, even in those difficult *kanji*. Koji asked several passers-by. No one knew the real name – but they could quote a nickname. It was called Job Centre Street – in part because there really is a job centre at one end of it.

I walked back to my hotel through the mass of well-lit underground subways beneath Shinjuku Station and the streets surrounding it. The homeless sleep there unmolested by the police. Sometimes, if they're lucky, a would-be employer wakes them up to give them a job. It's probably the only job centre Tokyo needs. Koji, ever the perfect gentleman, walked me back to my hotel, where I gave him my business card.

I could, I suppose, have gone on to investigate the nightclubs of the Rippongi area. These would have hostesses. But Japanese hostesses are quite often just that. It's not necessarily a synonym for something else. I know of a girl who went to Kyoto to work as a disc jockey and hostess and was taken out at £40 a time by men who only wanted her company at dinner.

In a sense, the Japanese are very straight and less into euphemistic synonyms than us. The card that offers you massages in your hotel room is quite literally true. What you will get if you phone that number is a proper Shiatsu acupressure massage *through* your unisex kimono. But what of the nice bellboys who carry your luggage with a smile and are not allowed to accept tips. What exactly is intended when they ask you with feeling, "Is there anything else I can do for you – anything at all?"

# Dublin

"You can call me Chris," she said, "Yes, Chris…I'd like that. And don't use the name of my hometown. You can say my father was American."

Chris is a prostitute. I met her down Waterloo Road by the side of the Burlington Hotel in central Dublin. Waterloo Road is one of a network of roads that I would describe as Dublin's red-light district. The locals, of course, would have it that there's no such thing – "It's a Catholic country – Dublin doesn't have a red-light district," I'd heard a man at the airport say. It's true that Dublin doesn't have one in the sense that Amsterdam does. There are no blue movie cinemas, peepshows, live sex acts, etc. Even brothels are thin on the ground. There was one in Mountjoy Square. It went out of operation after a political scandal, when a Protestant Right Wing senator was recorded on a video. The Irish press had a field day without mentioning any names, but those I talked to in the media felt that the whole thing had been trumped up – it was just too convenient politically. A woman who had worked nearby in a pregnancy counselling service above a massage parlour told me what the brothel was like – "as all the girls were single Mums the front room contained a crèche". Potential clients had to sneak past a room full of crying babies. Curiously, the men didn't find this an instant turn-off. Babies are okay. The one thing the Irish can't mix with sex is religion. The only place that hookers can't operate successfully is by St. Patrick's Cathedral.

Decades ago, the old red-light district was Monto, near Amien Street station – "Night Town" in Joyce's *Ulysses*. There's even a song that runs "Take me up to Monto". The area was closed down, or rather cleaned up, by the Legion of Mary between the wars.

These days, most of Dublin's sex scene is street prostitution. The girls on Fitzwilliam Square charge £40 for sex in a flat, or £100 per hour for whatever you fancy. They aren't left alone long. A few minutes' walking usually attracts a willing kerb-crawler. About half the girls on this beat are English. It's not such a difficult life. There are no pimps in the area and the police don't bother to harass them. I talked briefly to Marie, an Irish girl in her twenties – who told me the going rates. At first she'd said, "I've given enough bloody interviews!" Apparently, local students were always making a nuisance of themselves doing surveys.

Curiously, the better part of the red-light district overlaps with Dublin's Georgian Heritage Trail. Perhaps the reason that hookers choose this area is that few of the large houses are residential any longer. Half are for sale – the others are in process of being yuppified and turned into luxury offices. Consequently there are almost no residents to complain.

Fitzwilliam Square is the top end of the market – the easiest pitch. From Fitzwilliam Square it's downhill all the way: Merrion Square, Merrion Street, Leeson Street by the nightclubs, Baggot Street, Waterloo Road and Herbert Street in the area known as The Pepper Canisters (thanks to the shape of a church there) to the very bottom of the range by the canal-side, or worse still, Ben Burb Street. Ben Burb Street is named after a battle. All the prostitutes there look battle scarred. You can't even begin to ask them about their rates, because the only answer you'll get is "Go an' fok yerself" or threats of GBH. The girls here service passing truckers, sometimes spending all night in a parked truck.

Back in the middle range areas, girls can be aggressive too. It's understandable – talking to a journalist might lose them a passing trick. As one of them put it, "I write myself. We're not at all interested. I make my living out of prostitution." She was a formidable, masculine six-foot blonde with fishnet tights and a leather microskirt, oblivious of the iciness of Dublin nights. As the taxi driver I was with cruised back up the road, she and two of her friends ran at the car menacingly. By then we had picked up Chris. "Bitches," she said. "That lot would take on a policeman between them."

Chris was in the middle range. She charged "£15 or £20 for a toss, or £25 to £30 for sex". Neither she nor Marie talked of "French" (i.e. oral sex) being in demand with Dublin men. Chris was nervous about speaking to me at first. We had to drive to the outskirts before she would talk at length. The taxi-driver got a coffee for me and a can of orange for her, leaving us locked in the car. She wouldn't say what she had to say in front of a man and she wouldn't risk being seen talking in a cafe. "I suspect men." She'd been accused of "grassing" by certain people and suffered the consequences before. "Is this a set-up?" she kept asking us, nervously, examining the taxi-driver's license and my card minutely before getting down to her story.

At first, in front of the taxi-driver, she'd given some garbled fragments, muttering something about a "man doing time in jail for things he didn't do" or "I was gang-banged and raped up in the hills". Before she told me the full version, she made me promise to alter all the names of the people concerned, which I have done.

When we were alone, I asked her how she got on the game and the tale of her youth came spilling out. "I started young, when I was a baby. Nuns fostered me as a child in the Navan Road in Dublin. A couple came along, Pat and Maureen. I was three when he started at me especially round Christmas time. "You'll never go anywhere without me. You're my baby and we'll feed you." It nearly smothered me the way he used to lie on top of me. He was all brushy and tickly. I realised something wasn't right. He started doing things and I couldn't quite think what was happening to me. He kept going on. I always remember him touching me. I never knew who my Mum and Dad was. He used to say, 'I'll send you back to that place. Let me up you.' I was twisted and torn but I wouldn't let him up me." Chris stopped here to make some general remarks. "I don't miss love," she said defiantly. "A person has the right to choose their own way of life. I feel love for people – the whole people." It was a curious thing to say – curious that she could have retained love for anyone after the life she'd led.

"At Christmas," she went on, "I was playing with my Teddy bears and pianos. Maureen knew what was going on. I screamed out on the street – I was five then – 'I can't take it any more. He's having sex with me.' She wouldn't believe me. I went crying on and on and on. She still wouldn't believe me. 'He was at me again last night, your fokking husband.'" Pat's frequent attempts left Chris with broken sleep. He used her arse or his fingers at first. By seven, she wasn't a virgin any more. "I was seven when he finally broke me in." She went to the bathroom and stayed there wiping the blood away. When Maureen came in the morning, she said: "Go away from home, you're only a fucking whore." Chris had been happy when she came back until Maureen let her know they weren't her real parents. At that stage, Ben, aged eleven, Pat and Maureen's son, started to join in. "I can do what my Dad does. We can have you sent back and locked up." Maureen did in fact do that. Chris was sent to Lakelands Convent, Sandymount. She tried to tell the nuns what had happened to her, but that resulted in yet another ticking off. "Sister Frances had me transferred and told me I was a dirty little devil for telling the truth. I'm a true person and that's the way I'm going to stay."

Chris's next move was to Kilmacud detention centre – "like Bridewell" – where she was locked in a room with bars on the window. After two years in Kilmacud, she was brought to a hostel for older girls. They used to play cricket. She was given a job at 14, washing dishes in a nearby old peoples' home. Things were happier for a while, but Chris's troubles were far from over. She walked in one day at 3 p.m., after washing all the lunch dishes. "I heard moans in the grounds and I thought, Jaysus, there's a fokking cow in there!" It was no cow, but a lesbian nun enjoying herself with one of the girls in a curtained off section of the dormitory. Chris said: "So, this is what it's all about!" The nun threatened a further locking-up. Chris might have got away with it if only she'd been able to resist a further comment when she saw the nun returning from confession. "How did you get on?" she asked. Mother Brigid smacked her across the face, told her she was mad and had her locked up in solitary confinement for three weeks. "I found out they're all perverts. I find people in general, hypocrites."

After Chris's childhood, nothing went right for her for long. At fifteen she went on the game. Her choices were few with no qualifications, little confidence in herself and an education that had consisted solely of fierce discipline. There was a brief spell in England keeping a little shop in Camden after a small win on the pools. She acquired a boyfriend there who beat her up. She went on the game again and was gang-banged in a gift-shop in Shaftesbury Avenue by pimps who were trying to force her to take crack. Chris's indomitable will was not broken and she continued to refuse drugs. She just picked herself up after that incident and carried on. Curiously, Chris counted her spell in England as one of the happier parts of her life and bore no ill will to the English.

What every prostitute must fear most is that sooner or later she will run into a psychopath. That she will meet someone who will do her violence, not for any wickedly logical reason like wanting to keep her on the game, or to force her on to drugs – but gratuitously, just for the thrill it gives him. Chris met such a man years back

O'Malley seemed a little weird at first, but in a way that most prostitutes would consider useful. He didn't ask much for his money. He wasn't interested in sex. "He used to wank himself with baby lotion in front of me." Chris began to sense something was badly wrong the day he looked at her with absolute hatred and said:

"Your family…" as he tossed himself off. On the last occasion he paid her, he told her that he was going to have her followed by the police. Not long after, she was arrested when she was on her way to a dance and manhandled into a car. She wasn't even soliciting at the time.

From then on, Chris's life became a nightmare series of beatings, arrests and odd spells in mental homes when O'Malley tried to have her sectioned. Being remarkably sane, all things considered, she was usually released in a matter of weeks from the latter. O'Malley never laid a finger on Chris himself. He had ponces and ex-policemen and women in his pay. Chris knew where he lived and that he was rich, but was never able to find out what his actual profession was.

On another occasion, Chris was taken to the hills and gang-banged by O'Malley's ponces. One of them said: "I won't stop till I get you." A woman was present at the time and at several further beatings – an ex-policewoman called "Wexie" because she came from Wexford. Wexie explained, "We were sent to do the dirty work." The ultimate act of hypocrisy, Wexie held her hand in hospital and said: "Sorry Chris, it's not me."

"Every bone in my body is broken, but I put myself together again," Chris told me. She showed me the side of her mouth where several teeth had been smashed or knocked out and her hands covered in bruises and dried blood scabs on recent wounds. Her back, she said, was in the same state.

I tried to come at some motive for the beatings and all the rest. Was O'Malley a pimp? A dealer? A twisted moralist trying to force her to return to a life of washing dishes? Frequently the accusation was of "grassing" when she was beaten, although who or what she was supposed to have grassed, Chris either didn't know, or wasn't prepared to admit. Perhaps it was connected with her statement about a man in jail for things he didn't do. Or was the whole thing simply a case of mistaken identity? I put these questions to Chris. Her firm belief was that O'Malley was mad. "He wants me dead."

At this stage, in the switch of roles that every journalist dreads, Chris started to ask me questions. "What would you do?" "I'd run," I said. She had already told me that she couldn't go to the police, because police and ex-police were involved and she didn't know whom to trust there. Placing some sort of court order restraining O'Malley was also not an option. Considering he'd never laid a finger on her personally, even when he was a paying client, there was little that could be proved against him. Chris was too brave (or fool-hardy) to take my suggestion. "I'm tired of running." She took a sort of pride in being beaten but not broken. All I could suggest was that she left some part of her story with a solicitor she could trust, giving the names and addresses of O'Malley and Wexie and all the rest, just in case she was seriously injured next time they caught up with her in her frequent moves from one B & B to another in the suburbs of Dublin.

What struck me most forcibly about Chris's story was how society had failed her again and again. There are helplines for abused children now – at long last some of them will be believed. But what of the abused prostitute? Her position in society is very much like that of the child. Significantly, we describe members of her profession as "working girls" not working women, whatever their age. Like an abused child, she is the victim of figures of authority and her tale is seldom believed. While most forms of prostitution are illegal, the system is completely unable to help her. What is needed is a helpline akin to the one that exists for children, with individuals out there who are willing to listen, and, more importantly, willing and able to help.

Moralists will say that Chris and her type have asked for what they get by standing outside society. But what of O'Malley and others like him? Shouldn't society see that they get what they deserve, long before they turn down the path that leads to serial killings? Society must not be as tolerant of male sadism as it is. If psychos are to be stopped short and locked up before their violence turns to murder, then prostitutes, who are usually their first victims, but not necessarily their last, must be listened to.

# Cairo

WHEN YOU WALK the streets of Cairo by night, there's absolutely no sign of street prostitution. The Egyptians have a highly active equivalent of our vice squad. Whatever prostitution there is remains well hidden and underground. When a woman can get three years in prison if she's caught on the game, that's hardly surprising. On the other hand, considering that Cairo's all-night clubs with their jolly local music and dancing ensure that half the Middle Eastern male population comes there for a spree or a holiday, there has to be a big market for it, ready and waiting.

Cairo has more of a reputation than it deserves vicewise. A journalist I had met spoke of it having not one, but two, red-light areas. A doctor I talked to on the plane, a former native of Cairo, who was now working in AIDS research at a German university, gave me the addresses of the streets, warning me of the danger – knives, pimps, drugs, the lot. But his story turned out to be a pack of lies. Cairo's streets are as safe as any in the world are whether you choose the early evening or the small hours. Everybody wants it to be a Mecca of fleshly desires, but the truth is far different. In actual fact, its vice areas, its belly dancing and its prostitutes have fallen victim to a series of closedowns from early in the nineteenth century on.

In 1825, when the first medical school was established the bellydancers, who all then worked as prostitutes, were banished to Upper Egypt, i.e. further up the Nile. Ironically, Muhammad Ali who introduced this measure lent his name to the road that afterwards became their street in Cairo. Its continuation, and another vice area, *Clot Bey*, was named after his physician. By 1898, if an article in *The Strand Magazine* is to be believed, the city was again a centre of vice: "A most remarkable and revolting sight in Cairo is what is called the Fish Market. This quarter is inhabited by the lowest of the low. You can hardly call them men and women, they have sunk to such depravity. The males are in cafés, drunk with hasheesh – a sort of opium, which they smoke till they imagine themselves in battle, and sway sticks about in a helpless, stupid kind of way, just as if they were dreaming. The women stand or lie about the dirty, narrow streets, openly plying their horrible trade. At eleven o'clock they are compelled to go inside, and they sit behind iron bars inviting passers-by to come into their dark dens. The sight is indeed a

sad one. It would be hard to find women more utterly lost to everything womanly. They are as degraded as they are ugly. It is a wonder that such a scene is possible in a country under British rule." *The
Strand* goes on to hint that clean-ups were imminent – maybe they
happened and maybe they didn't.

Under Nasser, there was a lot of letting seedy rooms by the hour
to Arab visitors in the *Aguza* and *Zamalek* districts, but one major
change was made – the requirement that belly-dancers cover their
navels. This law is still in operation. Legal dancers wear an ordinary
evening dress, or at worst a top and skirt connected by a sort of fishnet area in black or pink. A few dancers flout the Law till they're
caught. I did see a bare navel in a tiny nightclub along the *Shari al-
Haram* (Pyramids Road). It is only in these small clubs and in some
hotels that prostitutes can operate with any chance of not being
picked up by the police. Belly dancers also run the risk of prison if
they move wantonly. I asked one Egyptian male to define what con-
stituted "a wanton movement". Would he demonstrate? He told me
that I was a woman, so I'd know better than he would. So why was
I asking?

Even if the small nightclub doesn't risk illegal belly dancing,
there will be a prostitute or two sitting at the back, eyeing up the
male customers as they come in. The usual price for a girl is
between one and two hundred Egyptian pounds (£17 to £33).

The main areas of prostitution used to be in Muhammad Ali
Street and its continuation, *Clot Bey* – the old Jewish quarter. In the
war, Opera Square, between these two streets, was also active, next
to the barracks that was there then. Red light districts often follow
the army. In those days there were regular medical check-ups.
Abdullah, a security man from a large hotel, told me of his first
experience, thirty years ago, in a famous brothel of the area, *Om
Simsim's*. (*Om* means "mother of". In a male-dominated culture,
women are often known by the names of their sons.) He went
upstairs in semi-darkness. He could just about make out that the
room was completely unfurnished. There wasn't even a bed. He
struck a light to see the girl's face and she got annoyed, thinking he
might turn her down. The price was about 50 piastres (8p) for one
come, whether you took a minute or hours. The girl lifted her gal-
labiyya and he took his trousers off. He didn't take long. When he
left, he realised his jacket had split down the back with the effort.

Muhammad Ali Street continued to function for a while after

prostitution became illegal. It was the home of the belly dancers. Now, even the name of the road has changed. The sign reads El Kalaa. Yet, everyone knows the place by its old name. There's a smirk on the face of any man you ask for directions.

These days, the average Egyptian prostitute is likely to be a country girl. Such a strong emphasis is placed on virginity that a non-virgin is almost certain to be unmarriageable anywhere in Egypt. Rape victims are lumped with those who've had sex by their own consent. In the country, a non-virgin also runs the risk of being murdered by her brothers. A great many country people carry guns and there'd be an "accident". As in almost any city, many prostitutes will be immigrants – Moroccans or Filipinos in this case. Rich Egyptians hire Filipinos as servants, who then become prostitutes. These days Filipinos are refused work permits in an attempt to shut down that particular branch of prostitution.

I was told also that there are two laws – Arabs and Egyptians can't take women to their rooms, but Westerners can. Just how this is policed I can't begin to imagine. There are also Egyptian prostitutes who've been discarded by their husbands. Saudis and Kuwaitis marry them, then when they're tired of them, they get sent back to earn a living any way they can. If they're uneducated, prostitution may seem to be the only answer. There are relatively few unskilled jobs open to women. Most shop assistants are male, most hotel workers also. A remarkable book called *Khul Khal* (golden anklet jewellery) details the humdrum existence of five Egyptian women in their own words. The stories were collected and written down by Nayra Atiya. None of these five women are prostitutes, but their tales reveal a cruel world where the major events of a woman's life are her clitoridectomy, her deflowering, births and bereavements.

Egyptian men might marry a widow, but they're not inclined to touch a woman who's been married elsewhere in the Middle East. There's a strong hatred between them and their more affluent Arab neighbours. "Saudis and Kuwaitis like to make love from behind so come to Egypt to try to buy mistresses from their families," I was told. "They get fucked in both holes, divorced, then sent back. We don't want women after they've had them – they have holes everywhere."

# Athens

ATHENS' RED-LIGHT district is centred around Omonoia Square – *Plateia Omonoias*. The square is a place where you can buy absolutely anything and especially anything that's slightly dodgy. At Easter you can get yourself a Paschal lamb that's fallen off the back of a lorry. Then there are the millions and millions of pairs of sunglasses. The glasses usually come in a Ray-Ban case, but there's absolutely no brand name on the spectacles themselves, unless it be "Made in Taiwan". When you walk around the square, one of the first things you notice is the ready availability of hard porn on every kiosk-cum-bookstall, down at child's-eye level. Similar magazines are sold elsewhere in Greece – in the tiny village of Marathon, for instance, near the bus stop, but nowhere else are they stocked in such variety and quantity. The bulk of the magazines are American or Americanised with titles – that betray their origins – *Color Climax. Inside Foxy Lady*, *Cum Shots* or *High School Anal*. I'm told that though many are imported, some are printed at Greek addresses with similar content and format. Magazine topics are specific – as well as the above you can buy *Masturbation, Sex Orgies. Sandwich*, *Teenage Sex, Transsexual, Homo Sex* or *Pissy*. I have a distinct feeling that most of them wouldn't make it past the English customs, as there's an unusual degree of emphasis on anal subjects and underage sex. A set of picture-backed playing cards is also available, entitled *Anal Poker*. The few titles available in Greek are mostly softer pin-up magazines apart from a few on sadomasochistic lesbian subjects.

The *Omonia* cinema advertises "HART CORE PICTURES" with two shows running continuously from nine in the morning until 3 a.m. The Star on *Leophoros Alexandrou*, just off the square, offers a similar programme. There are several other sex cinemas in the city but the shows advertised are less hard.

Greece is short of live shows. Nightclubs and discos in the area may have the odd striptease or go-go dancer – but that's about as far as it goes. *Cabaret Oasis* on *Plateia Karaiskaki*, at the other end of the broad *Leophoros Alexandrou* that runs down from *Omonoia*, has the frankest pictures outside its doors. But they're mild compared to Amsterdam. The club may not be intended to appeal to Greek tastes as it has titles outside translated into Arabic. The photos from the show outside are old, with curled-up corners and show a Dracula-like figure with cloak, false eyebrows and vampire's teeth, biting the nipples of the strippers. But there are no hours posted. I went inside one Saturday evening and asked the doorman. He told me in Spanish that the next dance show was at 2 a.m. on Sunday. Most of the hostesses at the bar are black girls in black or orange Lycra figure-hugging mini dresses. A great many of the drinking places labelled Pub in English letters also have hostesses in the streets off Omonoia Square and *Leophoros Alexandrou*. The style of dress is similar.

One thing that the Greek sex scene lacks is chatlines, although there's obviously a market for it. A piece in the *Athens News* said that dozens of Greeks had got themselves into grave financial trouble by running up immense debts ringing chat-lines in countries as far away as Australia.

If videos are more your scene, these are to be found near the Omonoia cinema and also in *Odos Aeolou*, a road that connects Omonoia Square with the old area of Athens, the Plaka. The titles would indicate a similar content to the magazines. The Plaka itself also contains a wide selection of jokey raunchy postcards with male nudes etc. amongst its tourist souvenir shops.

An Egyptian doctor once told me that an area not far from the Plaka – a maze of steps and tiny streets leading up to the Acropolis – was the best spot for prostitution. His statement might seem to be borne out by the litter of the local brand of condoms, *Stop*, near every park bench, and also by a large stone with an arrow daubed *Eros Kalos* (good love) pointing to a house nearby. But the house does not have the telltale red and yellow lights that mark a brothel in Greece. According to Greeks any prostitution in this area is strictly amateur. Though money may be extorted, it is usually just the price of a bed for the night or a meal. Sex will usually be al fresco on a park bench or against a tree. The girl will probably be backpacking her way round Europe and short on funds. She might be Australian, English or some other European. She's unlikely to be Greek.

Greek prostitution, on the other hand, is aimed principally at the Greek market. A prostitute has to be over 22 and registered with the police. She has to operate at a fixed address, not on the streets. She must have no criminal record and has to have two regular medical check-ups a month. Beyond that no guidelines are given. The prostitute I talked to was unsure what practices were or were not illegal. She was prepared to do absolutely anything for money – anal sex, sadomasochism, the lot – that is except having sex without a condom. In fact, she regularly used two. Other prostitutes, she hinted, were not as particular as she was and could often be persuaded to do away with protection for money.

Street prostitution still goes on outside the system. You are most likely to see women in the rather smelly *Odos Athenas* after the daytime market has closed. It's hard to conceive how anyone could feel erotically inclined in an atmosphere of stale fish, trampled cabbage leaves and squashed tomatoes, but the stray mangy cats and the prostitutes' clients don't seem to mind. *Odos Socratous, Odos Euripidous, Odos Menandrou* and *Odos Satovriandou* are also likely streets. (*Odos* means "road"). They are all off, or close to Omonoia Square. *Odos Voucharestiou* is also a place where any passing man will be accosted. As this road verges on the exclusive *Kolonaki* area, with its designer shops, you might expect a better grade of girl – but most of the ones I saw there were middle-aged and unattractive.

Regulated brothels are a little difficult to find at first. Though they should have a small red light above the door and a larger yellow lamp that can be seen from a distance, there's one slight problem. Greek light bulbs, like Greek lavatories, door handles, locks, switches and showers, don't always work...

I had extorted a promise of a trip to a brothel from two handsome Greeks, one a good English speaker, but alas, they chickened out and stood me up. In the end, I went with an English student from the British School of Athens. He had spent time at Thessalonike University and spoke Greek like a native. My own Greek is part Ancient, part Berlitz phrase-book and part one-usefully-obscene lesson from a Spartan celebrating the early hours of last Easter Sunday in bed with me. Though the obscene words might have come in useful, the rest would never have stood the test of an interview with a prostitute who spoke no English.

The legal brothels in the centre of Athens are in *Odos Euripidou, Odos Menandrou* and *Odos Phyles*. Most large towns in Greece will have one. That at Knossos in Crete, an archaeologist told me, is exceptionally rough. A Greek brothel consists usually of only two girls working from a hotel apartment. They live elsewhere. Brothels that are open over 12 hours – anything up to 24 – employ two different shifts of girls. As you might expect, they are charged a high rent. Trade is seasonal – winter being the time when Greeks feel at their randiest. Religious festivals are just as busy. August, the time when most of Athens goes on holiday and the running of the city falls apart, is the least busy month. Sometimes girls decide to shut up shop and go on holiday to one of the islands together, spreading their legs and showing their cunts to the sailors and tourists on the boats with jokey come-on offers of sex.

Sometimes one girl operates as a Madame and takes a cut; sometimes they just share expenses equally. The woman I talked to also had a shy girl on the door to let in clients. She was dressed in a loose sweatshirt and cotton trousers. The prostitute only wore a tiny black lace body stocking which could be slipped off or down easily.

One of the things that hit me when we first entered the flat was the heat. I endure heat well. The day's temperature had been up at forty degrees or so, but this felt hotter. I ran with sweat all over the moment I went in. The light inside was violet-tinged. There was little furniture: just three chairs for waiting customers and a coffee table with an ashtray – most Greeks are chain-smokers. On the inside of the door, several nude photographs of girls were stuck on the rippled glass panels. There were Art Deco posters on the walls including a reproduction of an advertisement for an old production of Turandot, a more modern picture of a girl in a swimsuit and some plastic flowers surrounded with a heart. American pop poured out of a speaker on the wall.

For the purposes of this article I'll call the prostitute Marina. She was welcoming and offered a ten-minute interview between servicing clients. She was more suspicious of my translator than me. We stayed for about an hour, in fact. The shy girl on the door was sent to prepare us iced coffee frappés – a welcome touch in that hot atmosphere. During that time Marina had four clients but refused many more. I was slightly surprised at the quickness of the men and timed one – two-and-a-half minutes. The others were probably not much longer. It made me realise how lucky I've been finding Greeks who took three or four.

There was no price set as such for hand jobs, but I would suspect that the sex was little more in that time. Blowjobs were 2000 drachmas (£6) straight sex about £8 as long as you didn't take more than five minutes and anal sex £30. In fact, for that amount you could have half an hour of whatever you fancied. She had only once had a lesbian client, though. Apparently, the commonest Greek kink amongst male customers is pretending you're married to the prostitute and having a quarrel followed by sex. Some Greeks also like to be tied down. She had from five to thirty clients a night, she claimed. It might have been an underestimate.

Most of the sex was naked as far as the prostitutes were concerned. Marina sometimes walked back from her client with nothing on, or in the act of rolling her body stocking back up. She had an extremely good body, but her face was older-looking with a slight cast in one eye. Her hair was bleached blonde, shoulder-length and crimped.

Marina's clients' ages ranged from 12 to 80. The Greek age of consent is 18, but she figured that if a boy could ejaculate that was okay. She charged less, took longer and was extra kind to get the young virgins hooked. My translator decided to ask a question of his own – one I'd never have thought of asking because I prefer to find out the facts about prostitution in different countries, rather than going into a prostitute's individual responses. Had she ever enjoyed it with any of her clients, he asked. Rather than the verb for fucking he used a Greek expression meaning to make love. She had never made love with her clients, she told him severely. She'd never enjoyed it with them. She was acting. She was an actress that's all.

While we sat there with our coffees several men came inside the door, usually in twos, looked around then fled. This was quite usual, Marina explained: Greek men were shy. She also threw out several clients. If she instinctively didn't like the look of one and felt he might cause trouble, he was out. Greeks are often racist. Most of those who failed her test when I was there looked perfectly harmless to me. I noticed that most of those who were given the bum's rush were Albanian or Asian, perhaps Filipino. One of those who left at her request had a large moustache and might have been Turkish. He kept coming back, she said, even though he was thrown out every time. Perhaps that was his kink.

The clients Marina serviced in the time I was there were all young – about twenty – and reasonable-looking. In fact, two of them I could really have fancied out on the street – that is, before I knew they only took two-and-a-half minutes.

In spite of throwing out more than half her clients on sight, there were frequent problems with violence, usually over money. Marina kept a German Shepherd behind the scenes to deal with awkward customers. I forgot to ask if he was allowed to join in for an extra few thousand drachmas. Sometimes she also called the police when the violence got out of hand. They were always very helpful. Her nearest scrape had been with an Englishman who had tried to strangle her. He had come in, asked if she was a transvestite, then gone for the throat when she dropped her body stocking to prove otherwise and asked him to leave. I suppose that explained her suspicion of my English-born translator. Though his Greek sounded Greek enough, his blue eyes and blonde hair gave him away.

Marina was cagey when I asked for amusing anecdotes. Even though I said I didn't want names, she told me she felt it was unprofessional to talk about her clients, except in a generalised way. She was open-minded and didn't want to criticise different forms of sex, she said – homosexuals, anal sex, whatever. It was people's own business. She did, however, say that she believed that Greece had become totally perverse in the last decade or two. I tried to pin her down on what shocked her. In the main, it seemed to be the prevalence of open relationships.

The greatest demand in Athens with both Greeks and tourists is for transvestites. They charge five thousand drachmas – about £15. It's often hard to tell they're not beautiful girls. They usually are more depilated than your average Greek woman is and they are all on hormones to give them breasts. They are not registered workers in brothels in the same way as Marina. They have their photo on record with the police – that's all. A transvestite friend of Marina's dropped in for a chat while we were there. Marina rolled up his navy and white striped tee shirt to show a pair of tiny, perfectly formed breasts. He was about to unzip and pull out his cock to prove he hadn't had the operation, when my translator stopped him, alas. I've always wanted to see a hermaphrodite in the flesh. My translator explained later that, although he himself was what the Americans would term "absolutely het", he found himself in the curious position of fancying the transvestite before him with his tall, willowy body, pretty face and legs like Cyd Charisse.

Did Marina have a special technique to make men come quickly? I asked. They have to desire her to start, she said. She'd make them believe they were making love to her. Then she'd use a bit of oral sex and put her hand round their cock and balls as they went inside her. She demonstrated in the air with her fingers tensed and spread wide. My translator asked if she ever put a finger up their arse, but she said no. I asked if she had a special technique for making men come quickly during a blowjob. In my experience men take forever, luxuriating in that position. That's one case where I'd much prefer the act to take a mere two-and-a-half minutes. Marina sent her transvestite friend into the bedroom for a large plastic dildo to demonstrate her technique on. She took a condom out of its sachet and rolled it on. My translator commented that it was a heavy-duty type, made in Czechoslovakia. He'd used one once but never again. Apparently they're thick as an inner car tyre tube and lack all lubrication. Once the dildo was encased, Marina got down on all fours, laughing, with one hand on my knee. She looked rather attractive then as her face lit up with vivacity during the demonstration. I don't think she'd get away with calling what she did a blowjob outside Greece. What she did, in fact, was move her chin energetically up and down, occasionally flicking her long tongue round the dildo's plastic knob, for about thirty seconds. That, she claimed, was enough to make a Greek man come. In this country she'd be sued under the Trades Description Act.

My hour-long visit ended with a trip to the room where it all happened. Inside the light was rosy above the king-sized bed. There was a washbasin and mirror on a side wall. It looked rather more comfortable than the average Greek hotel room.

# Turkey: Istanbul and Izmir

ISTANBUL, LIKE MOST of the large world capitals, is composed of a series of smaller places that have amalgamated. The legalised brothel area lies across the Golden Horn, near the Galata Tower in *Karaköy* (black village). It is in the *Lalali* district. The streets are narrow and cobbled – impossible territory for a car. At the opening of a road named *Zurafa Sokak* there's a man selling mussels on a great aluminium platter in the middle of the street. On the right, there's a row of leather jackets for sale, strung up on the wall. On the left, there are bootleg music tapes and underwear including a vastly outsized leopard-skin leotard. Halfway down the road, there's the prison-like gate to the brothel area, with a tiny police office inside on the left. When I tried to stop and take a photograph, a large policeman leaped out at me with a cudgel.

I went to the *Cumhuriyet* opposite to rethink my strategy. (*Cumhuriyet* is a common name for bars and cafés – it simply means "republic".) The café is upstairs and the table by the window has a good view down into the brothel area. It's the table most customers choose to sit at. Although it was the first day of Ramadan – a rather bad season for the vice industry – there were long queues of men at every door in the streets across the way. Some looked strained and nervous; others chatted amicably with their friends. The houses were narrow, mostly three storeys with brightly-lit shop-window fronts. In one I saw a girl come to the door in a baggy short white tee shirt skirting black bikini briefs.

It's not usual to allow women, other than the workers, into those streets. The reason the guard gave was, "They might see naked women." You can see a lot more flesh in the average Turkish bath.

Street prostitution is illegal in Turkey and carries a fine of about £10. There's little sense to working the streets when the brothel area is well run with police protection at hand. An Armenian woman, Matit Manukyan, owns all the houses off *Zurafa Sokak*. She's rumoured to be the third highest taxpayer in Turkey and is immensely popular because of a colourful personality and her large donations to charity. She lives near London's Hyde Park.

Homosexuals are also catered for in the brothels – at least those who are happy with a transvestite. All the transvestites who go on the game have had the operation and have been re-registered with women's identity papers. Concealing your sexual identity is illegal in Turkey.

The men in the *Cumhuriyet* knew a great deal about their next-door neighbours. While I was there, a large round metal tray was filled with tiny glasses of tea and *elma çay* (a delicious apple tea). I saw it go down the stairs and across the street held high above a boy's head. It disappeared amongst the milling crowd at the brothel doors. Apart from selling teas to the ladies opposite, some of the men in the *Cumhuriyet* had also been clients.

Officially, prostitutes are aged twenty to thirty-five, but, occasionally, someone in her late teens forges identity papers to get work. There are also a few older women of forty or fifty who are semi-retired, but continue to live in their homes, taking the odd trick for old time's sake. Only women live in these streets. There are no families, no pets, and no children.

About 15,000 men pass through the area every day – it's open from 8 a.m. until 11, or sometimes 1 a.m. At religious festivals it's often quieter. It's up to the women whether they want to work on those days or not. Many of the men walking in the area are simply onlookers and passers-by who've come with friends. If they decide to become a client, they pay about £5 at the door of the house of the prostitute they've chosen. When they go upstairs with her the rest of the bargain's made. The price of straight sex or relief massage is 100,00 Turkish lire (£7). A man can have one or more girls, or perhaps pay to see a lesbian act if that's the girl's speciality. The only thing there seems to be no demand for is SM. For oral sex a prostitute can charge anything up to a surprisingly high £100, according to my informants. The prostitute sells her client a condom to wear and she has regular check-ups. Usually she takes her clothes off for sex and washes herself after. The bedrooms have en suite bathrooms, but bidets seem, generally, to be unknown throughout Turkey. A woman's average earnings are twenty million lire a month, or about £2,000, after paying her dues. That would go an awfully long way in a country where you can get a tolerable hotel room, or eat a plate of kebabs and get drunk, for £5.

I was determined one day to enter the brothel area and see it all for myself. I had two alternatives. Either I could contact the police and ask permission officially, or I could try to pass myself off as a man. I decided the latter would be more fun, having been told by a friend and resident of Istanbul that I could probably pass for a "bent

Turk", the sort who was after a transvestite, if I concealed my hair and wore trousers. I could even wear lipstick and carry a handbag, he said. In the end I went for a straighter look and wore heavy walking boots, a grey flying suit covered by a man's khaki shirt and a tweed jacket. The jacket had square shoulders and the material was so heavy that it flattened out my breasts admirably when I wasn't wearing a bra. I took the colour out of my cheeks with foundation and powder and thickened my eyebrows slightly with a brown pencil. I wore no other make-up. My hair was thoroughly hidden in an U.S. army forage cap, set rakishly on one side. The whole ensemble had a military air. Being tall, I could pass for a foreign soldier, albeit a slightly bent one.

On my second visit I approached the brothels from the bottom end of *Zurafa Sokak*, opposite the Adabank on *Kremlati Caddesi*. A man was selling green chilli sandwiches to potential clients before they climbed the cobbled street. I tried some Turkish chillies later that night, assuming they must be weaker than other ones, to be sold in this way. They weren't. They nearly blew the top off my head and I had to drink a pint of beer fast to put the fire out.

In my discreet military-style drag I had no trouble getting by the policeman at the door. There are supposed to be two on duty, plus several plain clothes ones, mingling with the crowds. At first I thought that an upright posture would make me look more masculine, but soon I realised that most of the men inside were slinking, lurking and drooping, so I did what came naturally too.

The decor of the houses was not particularly interesting. One of the first on the right has stencils of mermaids on its tiled walls. Another house further down has a girl's name in lights, but few of the other women had bothered to do anything. I suppose that non-owners don't feel like investing much in special furnishings. About the only sexual element in these rooms is the stairs that lead suggestively to the bedrooms above. The women often stand on the stairs – either to give a hint to prospective customers, or perhaps just to save a minute on the way up. The bottom storey of every house has a large window, but the girls are much more discreet than those in Amsterdam are. Most wear ordinary clothes rather than underwear – low-cut tee shirts and short skirts or dresses. If underwear was worn, it was of a rather covering, unseductive type – a heavy-duty bra and half-slip, for instance. One rather prim-looking blonde in a dress wore glasses. She looked the type to appeal to a man with screw-your-secretary fantasies.

While walking as a man amongst men, I couldn't help wondering which woman I'd have chosen, if I'd had the wherewithal and the inclination. The secretary-type was prettier than some. Most were very obvious, with heavy breasts and hennaed or bleached hair. One of the bleached blondes took a shine to me: "I fuck you nice!" she offered. She'd have had a terrible shock if I'd gone upstairs and she'd found I didn't have as much as a salami down my pants.

About halfway down the first street, a crowd of men standing on the pavement opposite one of the houses attracted my attention. Obviously something special was going on. There were three women inside – one of them was dancing slowly and majestically to a tape of Turkish music. Turkish music is slightly like Greek but better – no bazoukis, but a distinctively oriental sound made by a clarinet-like wind instrument. It's hard not to move to it.

The woman who was in the centre of the floor was the fattest person I've seen in years. She reminded me of the curious squat, Anatolian fertility goddesses that turn up in every Turkish archaeological museum. They are some of the earliest representations of women – ancient fertility symbols. This living example must have been roughly a metre and a half round breasts, waist (if you can call it that) and hips. Her dancing was more of a slow shaking made by a slight movement of the shoulders and stepping from one foot to the other. She was wearing a tight pale peach leotard or swimsuit. With every movement, the cellulite reverberated like a huge milk jelly. It was a truly riveting sight. I couldn't take my eyes off it for five minutes. I could see the attraction for the crowd. If you were coming to *Karakoÿ* for a one-off experience, she might be the answer. It would be like having the Mother of all Mothers.

All the major cities in Turkey have brothel areas similar to those in Istanbul. I toured those in Izmir, after hours, in my normal dress and interviewed the chief of police who controlled them. This area, out of the centre, is known as *Tepeçik* (little hill), which has almost become a synonym for brothel locally. Modest souls tell their taxi driver to take them to *Yeni Sehir* (new town) – the place's other name.

Unlike *Karakoÿ*, *Tepeçik* is not owned by a woman. All the houses are individually owned – some by the girls who work there, some by men. One woman owns seven, though. There are several streets of brothels leading from a grilled gate which is closed for custom at

11 p.m. and opens again at 10 in the morning. There's a notice at the door saying that no drunks will be admitted. There are several policemen on duty at the control box – a comfortable building like a potting shed with stools, desk and a television. On the right a grim reminder – there's the hospital where girls receive their weekly check-up. In total there are 120 houses and 374 girls, including seven or eight transsexuals.

When the humans have stopped, the streets are full of copulating cats – tabby, black or longhaired Turkish. There's a lot of caterwauling. Some of them were using the bins outside the kebab shops or cafés. There are several fast food shops and one that sells low-grade underwear, tee shirts and swimsuits, mixed in amongst the brothels.

I walked past the houses. Some of the owners had closed their curtains or put out the lights. Most of the lower rooms reminded me of dolls' houses. They were set out as living rooms or bedrooms behind the glass shop window. Some had chintz three-piece suites or beds with heart-shaped scatter cushions. Some were bathed in lilac, red or rose-coloured light. Most of the prostitutes had disappeared for the night, although a few were watching television. One stood at her door. I'm told that one of them who was holding a kitten (obviously pets are allowed in Izmir) offered me an interview. There was one slight problem – she only spoke Russian.

Inside the brothels the names of the girls are displayed on the walls. The starting price in Izmir is the equivalent of £3 for straight sex. A higher price for other services like fellatio can be negotiated with the girls. One girl once earned about £140 in two hours – quite what for, it would be interesting to know. As in Istanbul, there is no demand for sadomasochistic practices.

The daily turnover of customers in Izmir is astounding. Some girls, I was told, can service one hundred men a day. It's enough to make you walk bandy even thinking about it. At £3 a trick, though, quantity is certainly needed – the girl has to pay rent out of her earnings if she does not own her house.

There's a rule on the gates that says drunks will not be admitted. Perhaps because of this, there is remarkably little trouble. There's never any real violence, but occasionally there are verbal quarrels about money, or if a client demands an unusual position or anal sex. Some clients wear condoms, some don't. Izmir is a port and the area services passing sailors as well as locals. American sailors visit by the shipload with their own military police to keep them under control.

Most of the women had retired to sleep or watch television by the time I had my tour. The few that were still about looked darker than those in Istanbul – some might have been gypsies. Girls and clients must be 21 or over. There's no upper age limit, but if a woman ceases to get clients she's retired and moved out. Younger women sometimes leave to get married.

When I'd finished questioning the chief of police, or rather when he was tired of answering, I was invited next door for a tour of the police station. It was a listed building – the Turks are getting keen on conservation – with blue plaster roses in the ceilings and chandeliers. We drank tea and chatted beneath a gilt mask of Ataturk on the wall. As I left, a woman came back through the gate after a day off. She had dyed black hair and tight purple leggings. The police chief told me with respect that she could earn £5 a go.

# Tel Aviv

SEVERAL DECADES AGO the chief area of street prostitution in Tel Aviv was by the clock tower, near old Jaffa. These days, it's on the Tel Baruch beach and up the pot-holed dirt track by the Mandarin and Colony hotels. Hopeful motorists drive out to choose a girl for a quick fuck in the back of the car.

The prostitutes accost the passing cars hopefully, Once they've left the Colony Hotel, it's a no through road that ends in the beach or a car park. Everyone's there with a purpose. I was with an Israeli writer. My presence didn't stop him being accosted. Seeing two people in the car, a girl shouted, "Do you want an orgy?"

Standing around all night is a wearying business, so some enterprising girl had made a sort of improvised sofa out of old car seats beneath a sun umbrella. At a pinch, it could be used for sex, if someone's car didn't prove big enough for an orgy.

There are no streetlights. The month before I visited, a woman was murdered on the beach. The police were still looking for the killer. There had also been several muggings.

Half the prostitutes there, the glamorous leggy ones, turned out to be transvestites – only the deep voice gave them away. The clothes left little to the imagination and allowed easy access. The best-looking transvestite was lounging in a low-backed black shiny leotard, cheeks of the buttocks hanging out, talking at a van window and bargaining with the driver. Other prostitutes wore baggy tops over bikini pants, miniskirts or shorts. Two women had their sweaters rolled up and both breasts out. One was stamping up and down and looking very large and Russian. (For a while, the Russian Mafia imported girls to Tel Aviv, not telling them quite what sort of work they were going to…but that's been put a stop to.) I asked another bare-breasted woman if I could take a photograph. "*Lo, lo, lo, lo!*" she screamed in horror (*Lo* is "no" in Hebrew.) For a woman who had both tits out, she had suddenly turned remarkably modest.

There's still a small scene operating near the old area in Tel Aviv, at the end of Hayarkon Street. Chayah, who keeps a bar there, talked with regret of the old days, when every bar and was crowded with girls. The area stayed open till midnight at least, some clubs even later. TV celebrities came to drink champagne and sample the ambience, not always the girls. The usual charge for sex was one hundred dollars. A cheap hotel room could be found nearby for about ten dollars.

About five years ago, the new mayor decided to clamp down on all this. The licences of many bars were not renewed. Some changed into coffeehouses, but many businesses went bankrupt as a result. Chayah's own bar did not look too healthy. We were the only customers in a long while. In the old days, there were strippers and entertainers in some of the clubs. Now Chayah's bar's only attraction is Tommy. Tommy is a charming little dog – somewhere between a Schipperke and a Chihuahua in looks. Chayah described him as a Pinscher. Tommy sits on a cushion near the door and can be persuaded to sing to customers. He does not have much sense of tune.

Chayah felt that the call-girl system was a poor one. She had sense to her arguments – you could, by chance, call your own daughter, your student, a girl soldier, or simply someone who wasn't your type. In bars, people had time to talk first and be attracted.

There are still a few girls working the stretch where Hayarkon Street joins *Kikkar Bet Be-November*, which leads into Allenby Street, a fashionable shopping area. The most successful pick-up point seems to be outside the new Bagel bar on the corner. It's a place where men and girls have every excuse to loiter before they strike a bargain. The price for sex has dropped considerably – these days it's only ten dollars. The clients are usually Arab immigrants, soldiers, building workers and a handful of religious Jews. The religious ones made the best customers, I was told.

There's no demand from clients for anything other than straight sex. Men are usually quite happy to have a drugged girl. Condoms are rarely used – addicts are careless with their lives and many customers try to insist on unprotected sex. The business goes on seven nights a week. An addict's habit, and the need to finance it, can't stop for the Sabbath. Prostitutes often pull no more than three customers a night, but may pick their pockets as well to make enough money to buy drugs. Some of the girls have pimps. The pimps are not pushers but addicts themselves.

The better-class girls moved up-market to become escorts or work in massage parlours, five years ago. Massage parlours offer a wide spectrum of sexual activities and are mostly open twenty four hours a day. Charges start at about sixty shekels (£15). Escorts can charge from two to five hundred (£50 to £125) depending on their level of looks and the number of hours spent with a client. When I asked about them at my hotel I was given a brochure called *Tel Aviv Today*. The back pages contained pictures of pretty escorts who work in various clubs and massage parlours. These services cater for tourists as well as local businessmen. The man on the desk assured me that male escorts could be provided also.

For those who prefer the solitary act, or wish to add a little spice to their marriage, Tel Aviv has ten sex shops. I visited one in the *Dizengoff* shopping centre. The shopping centre, named after Tel Aviv's first Lord Mayor, is full of coffee shops, boutiques and almost everything you could want to buy. Its air-conditioning makes it one of the chief shopping places when the streets become unbearable in summer. The different levels are connected with ramps and escalators. The sex shop lies on the second level, tucked in between a dentist's and a bridal boutique.

Israeli law decrees that no goods be displayed in the windows. The glass looks frosted and there are closed Venetian blinds inside. Anyone who enters must be over 18.

The Dizengoff Centre shop is one of a chain of five. It has been flourishing for the last nine years. Most of its customers are male and the bulk of its revenue comes from the busy video exchange. Most of the goods are imported from Germany and Holland. The shop has many Arab customers, young soldiers, etc – a few strict religious Jews also. Judaism seems less down on sex than Christianity is.

Away from the videos, the other half of the shop is given over to magazines comic items like china boobs, willy-warmers, condoms coloured to look like pink mice or green ghosts and sex aids. The sex aids range from pseudo-medical sprays and creams, through a small range of studded black leather bondage gear and vibrators up to life-size dolls. Down on a bottom shelf a plastic prick waits surrealistically on the centre of a cushion.

There are no legal restrictions covering anything on sale inside the shop. Out on the street, the censorship level is much higher. Earlier in the day I'd seen a poster for a faintly blue film where six pictures showing a couple had been edited behind the glass. Everywhere you'd have expected a woman's nipple to appear, you saw only a tiny square of white paper held on with two staples The effect was infinitely more kinky than any nudity could have been.

What struck me most about the contents of the shop was the

impressive array of sex dolls of various types. The better models cost around £90. When the shop had a smaller range of dolls, a customer demanded one with blue eyes. Not to lose the sale, the manager took one into the storeroom and inked hers in. Next day the customer came back complaining, "When she went to bed with me she started crying…" From then on blue-eyed dolls were always kept in stock.

I haven't seen such a large selection before, even in Amsterdam. There's everything from *Chinese Sex Girl*, perfumed to "smell like a real woman" to *She Male Doll*, a hermaphrodite with "Realistic Vibrating Penis and Strong Breasts". The latter is imported from Germany. Most of the female dolls carry guarantees that they can "hold up to 250lbs", which brings to mind visions of an 18-stone man humping his plastic lady.

The most expensive item in the shop (at approx. £180) was *Ms Perfection* who offers "double pleasure" with both anal and vaginal vibrators inside her perfectly formed orifices.

For the same price as the more ordinary dolls you can get an extra special designer vibrator –"Six inch realistic". It's "hand coloured and detailed to capture every vein, bulge and crease of a real erect cock". It "comes (sic) with its own designer pouch". If six inches is not enough, you can opt for *Jeff Stryker* – "these balls move when squeezed. Incredibly awesome in size. Moulded directly from Jeff's erect cock!" As an ex art-student I'd have been interested to know quite how that was achieved. How many cocks would stay erect under a dollop of clammy plaster of Paris?

The world of the sex shop is a little unreal compared with what goes on out on the street. Chayah had suggested that we return at midnight to have a coffee with her in one of the shops near her bar, promising us the sight of all Tel Aviv's addicts coming in for a fix. For a city of half a million inhabitants, the drug problem is an extremely small one. Both drugs and prostitution are illegal, officially, but the police don't harass anyone concerned. I saw several police cars drive by between midnight and two in the morning, but they were only keeping an eye to make sure that things did not get out of hand. The police only interfere when there are complaints. They would much rather know who the addicts, pushers and prostitutes are and where they can be found than drive the problem underground.

Round the corner from the bagel bar, there are two old cafés that sell everything from Israeli specialities like falafel and salad in a pitta, to gateaux and coffee. The prostitutes and pushers sit here to unwind and chat. The healthier addicts manage to down a meal. Some clients turn up the same time every night for a packet of pills and a plate of falafel. Everybody knows everybody. I was beginning to recognise various people from earlier, including a fat middle-aged man with a striped Benetton tee shirt clinging to his potbelly. I'd suspected him of being a prostitute's client, earlier, but he turned out to be the chief drug pusher. Another middle-aged man, a sort of latter-day Gladstone, goes there solely for philanthropic purposes He owns a restaurant in Jaffa. He's trying to get into politics to get more rights for these women. He's not the only person concerned with this. A woman lawyer, whose daughter had been raped, has started an association for prostitutes.

The girls who come to the man in the striped tee shirt look spaced-out like zombies. One or two are shaking. One in a crocodile-print lilac miniskirt is talking in a quarrelsome way about money. She's like a battered, emaciated version of Cher.

I checked with Chayah which prostitutes were transvestites and which were women. I've never yet been deceived into believing a transvestite was a woman, but I found myself imagining that some of the women were transvestites. After military service a young Israeli woman often has a kind of wide-shouldered, healthy-looking beauty. When that particular kind of tall, muscular shape is hit by drugs and poor eating, it becomes etiolated and masculine. Two of these women looked just like men with breasts.

The real transvestites in this area have no hope of affording the operation. It's seldom attempted in Israel. A transvestite would have to save for a trip to Switzerland and about three months off work afterwards. But an addict spends everything that he earns.

Chayah passed some comment on everyone as they arrived. Most of the girls were Israeli, but one was a Bedouin. She is the only Bedouin girl in the profession in Israel, Chayah told me proudly. She looked more like a female bricklayer in her very unwhore-like jeans and checked shirt. She had a rather plain face curtained by luxuriant curly black hair, stiff as a horse's, and her bottom was as vast as a Victorian bustle. But then, at least she didn't look like an addict.

Since the Holocaust, most Jews have become, if not thoroughly religious, at least proud of and knowledgeable about their heritage. Once it was known that I was writing about the red-light district, a discussion of Biblical whores ensued – Rahab and others. In Israeli schools, I was told, Rahab is explained euphemistically as a seller of food (rather than of sex). *Zona* is harlot in Hebrew. The syllable *zon* occurs in *mazon*, the word for food. Thus, a far-fetched and slightly improbable etymological explanation is possible to keep the kids in ignorance for a few years longer.

Between midnight and two, some of the Tel Baruch girls came to join the party. There was almost a family atmosphere around the tables. I'd always imagined a drug-passing area to be thoroughly unsafe, but this seemed positively cosy. The nearest the street came to experiencing violence was when two young Russian men started a fight and a glass was broken by accident. They could hold their vodka, but were unused to the Maccabee beer. They were dealt with compassionately. A man from the café helped one off in one direction, a woman helped the other. It was all over peaceably in no time at all. The proprietor tactfully took us inside to eat while the mess was cleared up. We went outside for coffee later. As the night went on, a small taxi rank built up, taking the citizens of Tel Aviv back home with their pills and packets. A car full of Orthodox Jews in black stopped and they were supplied. Chayah commented that most of the strict religious Jews turn up later – between two and four in the morning.

There were other people hanging round the restaurant chatting now – two deaf and dumb mutes. They were not prostitutes, clients or pushers. The woman came up and held an animated conversation in sign language with Chayah. She gestured that she'd just broken her *Mezuzah*. A *Mezuzah* is a tiny container that holds a written scriptural blessing. You find them nailed to the door of every house. Breaking one and losing the writing must be a bad omen.

The crowd around me could have been straight out of Villon's poems. I was reminded also of a strange early American film, *Freaks*. Everyone in that film was disabled and working for a circus. They ganged together to amputate the legs and tongue of the beautiful trapeze artist who had married the dwarf for his money. She became one of them.

While the disabilities were not half as extreme as those in *Freaks*, the people at the tables were all outsiders, visually different, treading a fine edge between crime and respectability, masculinity and femininity The more I sat with them, the more I sensed their infinitely strong camaraderie.

By two o'clock there were no new faces amongst the women. There were probably only a dozen prostitutes all told, including some we'd seen at Tel Baruch. A little old lady emerged from the back of the café. She looked timid and kindly. She had a brief chat with some of the girls and Chayah before retreating into the kitchen. Her cheeks were lightly scarred – by old acne perhaps, and she had a massive gathered-looking goitre on the right side of her neck. When she had gone, Chayah told us that the old lady and her sister had been survivors of a terrible experiment by the monster Mengele. She didn't need the money working there, but came every night for the company in the small hours, to avoid being left on her own.

# Brussels

UNTIL A FEW years ago Brussels had three red-light districts. These days, it's more like one and a half. It's not that anything's been made illegal – prostitution's been illegal there for a long time anyway – it's simply the state of the Belgian economy. The first thing the unemployed, or poor, cut back on is the sort of sex they have to pay for.

The one business that's booming is the peepshow. The machines take 20 or 50 Belgian Franc pieces (40p or £1) for a couple of minutes or so of viewing time. You can choose to watch either a video or a live act. I was stared at with a look of the utmost disgust when I changed a note to try one of these shows at *Erotica* in the *Rue du Cirque*. The man on the desk is cunning. He makes sure he never has any 20f pieces, so clients who haven't come prepared end up having to use 50 francs a look. Most of the live acts are just a woman on her own. The one I saw wore an open leopard-spotted chiffon blouse and a bored expression. She went through a series of poses – half go-go dancer, half gymnast – running her hand across her fanny from time to time, before the shutters came down. I wasn't moved to put in a second 50 franc piece – I can always look in the mirror if I want to see that sort of thing, although I do not have the added refinement of a small puma tattooed on my left buttock.

Since last year, live double acts have become legal. They are fairly uncommon though. They are usually housed in a special booth with an entry price of 250 Belgian Francs (£5). There is one at the *Erotic Peep Show* at the bottom of *Rue de Brabant*. As one of my informants put it: "Even an unemployed man can afford that."

Next door to the peep show, there's Brussels's largest sex-shop. There have been radical changes to Belgium's laws on pornography in the last few years. Before that, the videos and magazines available were so tame that many Belgians crossed the border to stock up. A sex-shop in Sluuis, just over the border into Holland, cashed in very nicely. Motorists would stop off, fill up the boot of the car, and then head back home again. Eventually, the government realised that the home market was losing money as a result. The authorities are still against paedophile material – the recent prosecution of a priest involved with children in such films brought public attention to the subject. Animal videos and sadomasochistic live acts are also not permitted. Only one of the black prostitutes in the windows had been dressed in the sort of gear that would imply SM might be her line – a black leather corset.

Gay pornography is allowed, but Brussels is, on the whole, too straight for it. Although I'd seen one transvestite, they're a rarity. There are none operating from bars. The only hope of finding a gay prostitute is in a disco. Brussels is far less gay than Antwerp. Antwerp, being a major port, needs to provide more for its sailor customers. There are many transvestites operating from "bars" there. There are also, a great many more "bars".

The central red-light area of Brussels where I had looked at the peepshow is dying fast. It once consisted of *Rue du Colombier, Rue du Malines, Rue du Pont-Neuf, Boulevard Emile Jacqmain* and *Rue du Cirque*. The latter road is the only one that now looks like part of a red-light district, but there's still a bit of activity around the clubs in *Rue du Pont Neuf* and *Boulevard Emile Jacqmain*. There are only a couple of windows left with women in. I caught an elderly prostitute's eye as I passed and she laughed and smiled. There were also two or three girls on the street plus one ugly transvestite. He had dreadlocks and a mini-skirt. He spoke to his pick-up in a rough bass voice – the only feminine thing about him was the skirt.

There used to be an array of tiny bars with windows full of girls in this area, but these were demolished to make way for larger buildings. Now, most of the trade here is done on the street – straight sex at a thousand francs (£20) plus a hotel room, unless it's done in the client's car.

The up-town area, the suburb of Ixelles, near the Hilton, is deader still. There were several clubs, but only one still seems to be open. The *Club Aloha* is next to the Anglican Church at the point where *Rue Capitaine Crespel* curves round to join *Rue Stassart*. Its narrow frontage almost looks like part of the lower storey of the church. On summer evenings, you can see a shocked vicar leaning out from a window almost above the club's door. The clubs in the nearby streets of *Rue des Chevaliers* looked thoroughly closed. Once, all these streets, together with *Rue des Drapiers, Rue de la Concorde* and *Rue de la Grosse Tour* formed another red-light district. Now, there's not as much as one ugly transvestite left walking the beat.

The bulk of the prostitution is carried on in the north of the city near the *Noordstation*, or *Gare du Nord*. You can find an ample choice of girls most hours of the day or night in *Rue d'Aerschot*, an unsavoury grimy road that runs along the side of the station. The whole area smells of pee. There are puddles of it in the gutter and by the station wall. Most of the girls now work twelve-hour shifts to find ten clients or so. Several years ago they only worked five to make the same money. Most display their hours and phone number in the window. About the only time you'd have difficulty finding a woman is between six and ten in the morning. At any other time of the day or night, you'll find twenty-five or so windows with a girl in underwear sitting in them. At the weekend, about half these girls are black, mostly immigrants, legal or otherwise, from Zaire. During the week, most of the girls are Belgian. The customers seem to vary according to the time of day. On weekend nights I saw a gaggle of nightmare clients, old with few teeth and a scattering of bristles on their heads. Most of them were wearing long pee-stained macs that had been slept in for years. By day, there were many more young men – lorry-drivers stopping off en route, etc.

Belgians insist that these establishments are bars not brothels. Each "bar" has a list of slightly over-priced beers in the corner of its window, but you won't find drinkers or bottles much in evidence inside. Some windows also advertise Durex. In the spirit of finding a euphemism for everything, the girls are called serveuses – barmaids. Sex usually takes place behind the bar and costs two thousand francs (£40). Other activities are by negotiation. A client might pay up to ten thousand (£200), occasionally, for something unusual with an extra special girl.

Belgian prostitutes must have something. Every time I saw a customer leave, he was wreathed in smiles and shouting greetings or promising to come back. On a weekday, *Rue d'Aerschot* is jammed with traffic. Some is just passing through into the city, but there's a sense that the drivers have chosen that route. A good many of those with vans, lorries or taxis are hailed by name from the doorways. Girls come out to wave at old customers as if they were long lost friends. The only person I saw slink away unsatisfied was a young Slav who'd been desperately trying to persuade a girl to drop her price to a thousand francs – all he had on him.

While the ordinary rents in this area are the cheapest in Brussels, bar girls pay the price of an expensive hotel room – upwards of £100 a night – for the use of their premises. The cost of the rooms could be brought down by sharing, but then the clients would have to be shared too. Some work alone, in other cases there might be several in a bar. Most girls clear about £300 a day once the rent is paid.

Officially, prostitution is still thoroughly illegal. The police pass through the area frequently. When they see a new girl she's brought in for questioning. She will not be charged – they are only interested in pulling in pimps. In French, pimps go by the colourful name of *maquereaux* (mackerel). It's pretty much impossible for a prostitute to live with a boyfriend in Belgium, if the police find out about him. He is automatically assumed to be living off immoral earnings. Drugs are also frowned on, although quite a few of the girls are on them. Some also live with a man who's a pusher or addict. The police descend occasionally on the bars and check identity papers – particularly those of non-European males.

There are also a few genuine bars in the road. These have large beer adverts on their frontage and there are no coloured strip lights. Most of the windows with girls have, by contrast, three neon strips, one violet, two red. The real bars where you can sit and enjoy a beer at normal prices all have Polish barmaids. The pay is small, but it's more than they could get back home.

Some girls slump in chairs covered with red fun fur, others pose more artistically on stools, stomach-in, tits out, Page-Three-style. Most of the black girls try harder. A few of the blonde Belgians exude serious boredom – they pick their legs, read a newspaper, or eat a takeaway while potential customers file past.

It's easiest to observe the decor in unoccupied windows that have just been vacated by their owners. Sometimes a guard dog or a kitten nips in and takes up the unoccupied chair. Sometimes the objects in windows are carefully arranged. A pair of unwearably high red patent stilettos lies casually in the window of the *Surfrise Bar*. Other props give a hint as to what nationalities would be welcome. *Yafo* has a Japanese blanket in the window. Elsewhere, you can only see a scatter of make-up brushes and a mirror beside an unused stool. Sometimes the objects defy explanation. Just round the corner, in *Rue Linné*, the girl had left behind a statue of Buddha, several soft toys and a half-eaten packet of Jaffa cakes.

*Rue Linné* is one of several roads that lead away from the Botanical Garden. All have horticultural names. *Rue Linné*, *Rue des Plantes* and the roads that intersect them – *Rue de la Prairie* and *Rue de la Rivière* – all have a scattering of "bars" with red and violet strip-lights. The windows are far less obvious though. Either there's no girl in them, or you can only half see her through net curtains. The only woman who was visible was discreetly dressed and looked about sixty – at least twice the age of any of the girls in *Rue d'Aerschot*. She had a large bosom and a blonde bouffant hair-do like Mrs. Thatcher's. *Rue Manlé, Rue Verte, Rue du Progrès* and *Rue Dupont* make up the remainder of the northern red-light district, although there's less in evidence in these streets.

As you walk through the area, you become conscious that it's a kind of Muslim ghetto. The houses are scruffy and poor. The shops mostly sell cheap clothes, food, perfumes and household goods from Turkey and Egypt. The people who actually live there – most prostitutes do not – all seem to be North Africans, Egyptians and Turks. It's a bizarre thought-provoking sight to see a thoroughly-veiled dumpy woman coming out of her door with her husband, right beside the window of one of the prostitutes who's wearing nothing but bra, knickers, stocking and suspenders and is bathed in rosy light. Each seems to avoid looking at the other, but do they ever, for a minute, wonder what it would be like to swap places?

# Mexico City

IN MEXICO CITY a red light district is known euphemistically as "a Pink Zone" – *Zona Rosa*. It's an area where tourists will find an abundance of bars and restaurants as well as a bit of prostitution on the side.

The two main streets for picking up a girl are *Parque Via* and *Viaducto*. I'm told there are a few under-age girls working there, but I didn't see any. The price for sex with a street girl includes the use of her room, or a cheap hotel. In *Viaducto* it's 200 dollars, in *Parque Via* it's 125. The girls are extremely health-conscious. Visiting charity workers have slammed the AIDS message home. Condoms are used for both straight sex and blowjobs.

I was told there were cheaper prostitutes – seriously old and seriously ugly ones – by the bus terminal, but I saw none. Maybe they were so old they'd all died off, or maybe it's just a male myth.

Apart from prostitution, there's no other sex industry to speak of. You won't find shops for videos or sex aids. Saunas and massage places are just what they say throughout Mexico, except in Americanised Acapulco. Neither are there any brothels or full stripteases, these days. The most you'll find is the odd topless bar. Until a few years ago there was table dancing, but even that's vanished now.

Prostitution in Mexico City operates either on the street, or from bars. You would have a very hard job finding a prostitute by day. Although prostitution's illegal in every shape and form in Mexico, the police take a fairly lenient attitude. The girls are not harassed – those who work on the street are simply moved round the corner if an important politician is about to drive through their part of town. In spite of prostitution not being legalised, girls are encouraged to register via the police with the Ministry of Health. They are granted a licence and take regular medical check-ups. This is part of the Mexican national policy regarding the control of Aids.

Several decades ago, prostitution was more open. There's an amusing painting by Emilio Baz Viaud in the *Museo de Arte Moderno*. It shows the *Calle de Cuauhtemotzin* in full swing at the beginning of the Forties. I couldn't find this alley on contemporary maps. Presumably it was in the *Cuauhtemoc* district which has now gone up-market – various embassies, including the British one, are sited there. The area devoted to prostitution has shifted slightly, but not too far. The most expensive girls operate in connection with the bars along Insurgentes – the main street that runs from the north to the south of Mexico City. The bars are clustered at the beginning of the south half of the road as it runs away from *Paseo de la Reforma*. There are a few transvestites who work there, but they're not widely in evidence.

I met Marianna in one of these bars – *El Dragon de Oro*. She was pretty in a typically Latin American way – extremely short with a pocket-Venus-style figure and luxuriant, curly, long, dark hair. She looked about twenty. She was wearing thigh-length black plastic boots with spiky heels, black hot pants and a red clinging stretch-nylon cropped top. The style of dress of the other girls in the bar was similarly tarty, several wore mock leopard hot pants, even one fat one – she was dancing. The only middle-aged prostitute there had a larger bosom. She had settled for a Basque-style top that showed more cleavage.

*El Dragon de Oro* looks exactly like a Chinese restaurant. On closer inspection though, the menu only seems to contain rather expensive drinks and the tables are littered with cards that tell us in Spanish and English: "Say Not at the Drugs". The music was a noisy disco beat. The men on the door show you to your table and also act as security in case there's any trouble. Violence is rare. Marianna had never suffered any problems. She believed it only came about when a girl went back on her side of the deal.

About twenty-five to thirty girls are attached to a bar. They are not paid and equally don't pay anything to the management. They are considered an attraction to customers. Whatever bargains they make are their own responsibility. Marianna said she charged anything from 600 New Pesos (about £150) up to double that, according to whether she needed to pay her rent or not. The other girls in the bar charged similar prices. Payment was for one come only and the client also was responsible for paying the hotel. This could be a further forty to one hundred New Pesos (£10 to £25). A client might spend anything from fifteen minutes to an hour having sex. Often she would have dinner with them first. Sometimes that was all she did, acting as a sort of escort. She only had one client a night. She usually worked a few hours – say eleven till three in the morning. Most of the men who picked Marianna were in their forties.

Some were regular customers. Other girls in the bar might attract younger men.

She had never been asked for anything kinky. All the men seemed to want was straight sex or blowjobs. She always used condoms for both activities as she was terrified of AIDS. Punters were mostly American, Japanese, Italian and Mexican. Marianna launched into a description of the different national characteristics. The Japanese are very fast, but nice. They often give a tip afterwards. Americans are slower. They always say "Thanks". The Mexicans are gluttons – more sensual, more hot – a lot of touching was involved. Italians liked different positions – sex in the bathroom, for instance. She felt more with Latin races, she said. At this point, I asked if she'd had any Englishmen. She had. "And what were they like at sex?" I asked. She turned silent and thought for a long while before replying that she couldn't remember!

I had visited *El Dragon de Oro* with a lawyer from the department that deals with consumer protection. He couldn't resist telling Marianna that he had, in the past, been responsible for closing the bar down twice. She responded by clapping his right hand to her breast. He was asked to feel how nervous that made her. He said that he couldn't feel anything. That was because her heart had stopped, she responded wittily. Evidently the hand on the breast had done the trick. Phone numbers were exchanged and a meeting was to be arranged. "Can you afford her?" I quipped sarcastically. "Oh, I'm only going to take her out to dinner," he said.

# Copenhagen

A COUPLE OF centuries ago, Copenhagen and Elsinore (Hamlet's place of origin) were thriving ports full of sailors' brothels. An eighteenth century inventory mentions a green parrot among a brothel's furniture. The bird was in the habit of saying: "Angel, let's go in the back and see my chamber."

In 1877 a series of regulations for the control of prostitution in Denmark began. Prostitutes were not supposed to operate anywhere near the Royal Castle and they weren't allowed to live with their children once the children had passed the age of four. In 1901, all brothels were closed down. In Copenhagen's Erotic Museum, on *Vesterbrogade*, there's an interesting photo of the last establishment, in *Didrik Badskjaers*. It shows floors strewn with sand and a collection of fat motherly women sitting round with their pet dogs. In those days, street prostitution was in *Holmensgade*, a road that links the canals near the port where ships leave for Norway or Sweden. In the Fifties, there was a brief revival of an amateurish form of prostitution. Good-time girls would pick up an American sailor in a Dixie Bar and spend the weekend with him, taking him round the best night spots – *Jomfruburet, City Bar, Evergreen, Silver Dollar* and *Maxim*. Only the Maxim Bar still seems to be in business. The girls were not in the strictest sense prostitutes. They went with their sailors mostly for treats and presents rather than hard cash.

Contrary to popular belief, prostitution is still illegal in Denmark, although almost anything goes in the way of magazines or videos. The average punter who wants to find a prostitute as quickly as possible will probably pick up a copy of *Copenhagen This Week*. The woman in the Tourist Office told me she was absolutely sick of male holidaymakers coming to her for advice on where to get sex – giving out the free brochure provided the simplest answer. The *Copenhagen By Night* section lists various clubs, saunas and escort services. The highest of claims are made. Beside a picture of a blonde in black lace underwear we are told: "Top class young ladies. Nice dressed and speak all languages." The Danes are certainly good linguists, but that's a bit of a tall order. Judging by the faces on the street, the languages tourists would be most likely to require are English, French, German, Spanish, Italian and Japanese. Most credit cards are accepted by the escort services that aim at this market. Some of the ads offer a quality that's not usually required – as well as being sweet, sexy, discreet and high-class, the girls are supposed to be "funny".

Street prostitution still exists of course, but there are relatively few women on the game. It's quite hard to tell a Danish prostitute from anybody else. She is usually tall and blonde, which is not as glamorous as it sounds, because she will probably be dressed in a pair of faded jeans and an old cardigan. Some of the girls look drugged, one or two are probably teenagers. There's a sense that almost none have bothered with their appearance – they wear little or no make-up and the hair is usually out of condition and untrimmed. The older women don't walk the street. There are just a few of them left sitting in little one-woman "clubs" marked with a rosy lamp or two and offers of massage or spanking. These women are usually fat with grey hair and tightly packed into puce or black stretch-velour dresses. A man would have to be seriously into mother-fucking to want any of them.

The red-light area is near the main train station, along *Istedgade* and some of the side roads that lead off it, mainly *Abel Cathrinesgade, Eskildsgade* and *Viktoriagade*. Where the area peters out, along *Istedgade*, there's a small shop, *Erol's*, where the tourist can buy an elaborately-modelled erotic Meerschaum pipe or a statuette of Priapus, if he can afford £150 for his own miniature work of art. The whole area's full of sex shops, tattoo parlours and clubs. Girls often loiter by the windows of the sex shops to catch a client who has just been turned on by the videos inside. All the street girls use the premises of clubs by private arrangement. The telltale sign that sex is available, or going on above a club, is small candles or night-lights in glass containers in the windows on the first floor. The candles are often red or blue. Most of the buildings in this area are four storeys high, but the upper floors contain only ordinary apartments.

Street prostitutes charge two to three hundred Kroner for straight sex (about £20 to £30). The customer pays 90 Kroner for the room (£9). If he picks a girl up in a bar at the better sort of club, he will pay more – about £50 for sex or £30 for fellatio or a hand-job. A full hour with a girl would be about £100.

Clients are a mixture of nationalities: tourists and Danes in the clubs, Danes and immigrants on the streets. There are a great many immigrants in the red-light area – Arabs, Turks, etc. Most of the Arabs congregate in tiny snooker dens mixed in amongst establishments with names like *Club Amour*. A couple of Iraqis I talked to told me that most of the Danish prostitutes were willing not to use condoms for a little extra cash.

Most of the clubs stay open all night. There's little happening before 8 or so in the evening. The area has another kind of life by day. If you see a prostitute in the morning, she's probably just popping out for a packet of fags or a carton of milk for her breakfast. The sex shops, some of which contain cinemas, are open, but you're more conscious of a wealth of greengrocers' stalls, many of which are kept by Turks. These have some of the largest, curliest, non-regulation cucumbers you could wish to see. If the EEC knew about them, they would certainly straighten them out.

The sex-shops have an enormously varied stock. At least half the customers are tourists from countries where less is available. The not-guilty verdict in an obscenity trial over *Fanny Hill* in the early Sixties opened the floodgates. The police did a few more half-hearted raids – the last, in 1967, emptied the shelves and English and Swedish material had to be imported to fill the gap. In 1969, pornography was officially "liberated". Denmark was the first country in the world to do this. Since those days, the police have not been a problem. They drive through the area but keep a low profile. The only raids are on clubs – either because they suspect drugs are being sold, or because there's been trouble. Denmark produces *probably the best lager louts* in the world – well, nearly as good as British ones.

Some clubs or shops advertise a "BIO". This is short for the old word "Biograph" and simply means that they have a cinema. For £4 or £5 you can spend most of the day watching hard porn movies. These are often described as "Non-stop sex-shows" but they are really only films or videos. Every shop lists its specialities outside – *Lesbian, Milkmaids, Oral, Piercing, Flogging, He-she, Bondage, Caning, Enema, Anal, Animal, Bi-love, Big bust*, etc. *Private Corner* also offers *Faust* movies – a source of great puzzlement to me until the proprietor told me he'd forgotten and put one German title in amongst the English ones. Faust is the German for "fist".

Gay men who're into pornography could have a wonderful time in Copenhagen. There's a large homosexual sauna with a cinema on Istedgade, as well as a specialist supplier in *Viktoriagade – Men's Shop, The Best Gay Place in Town*. The window contains magazines with titles like: *Run Little Leather Boy Run* or *Dungeon Master*, hundreds of condoms and jars of anal lube. There were so many whips, handcuffs and instruments of torture hanging from the ceiling grid, just inside the door, that I had to pluck up courage to enter the shop. When I did, the man behind the counter turned out to be sweet and gentle and answered all my questions. The building also contains a cinema and a dungeon. It's open until two in the morning, seven days a week. For a mere £5.50 you can spend fourteen hours watching movies or having a good sadomasochistic time in the dungeon with friends or strangers. It sounds like the best gay value in Europe.

There are just two rules in the shops and cinemas. Customers must be over-eighteen and the actors in the videos sold or watched must be over sixteen. One of the shops had some girls that looked younger on the magazines in its window. Interestingly, its manager was the only shopkeeper who claimed he didn't speak English when I went in asking questions.

Apart from under-age sex, everything else imaginable is allowable. There are Rape movies as well as a host of bestiality videos. Personally, I don't see much harm in videos of women being rogered by beasts, as long as the actress is properly paid and the animal's enjoying himself. I had figured that Great Danes would star in some of these videos, but I was staggered at the variety of other participants. *Animal Zoo* seems to have a photograph of an ant-eater sucking off a woman on its box – the picture was so murky, it was a little hard to tell precisely which beast it was. I asked an assistant in one of the shops that specialised in bestiality what other animals were featured. "We've got lots of horses and dogs," he replied, "that's normal. But then, there are things like this…" He produced a video from behind the counter called *Eels for Pleasure*. Bestiality videos sell very well – people buy them for the shock value more than for anything else. Customers told him that they would bring one out at a party. The prices of videos start at about £6.50 with large reductions for multiple purchases.

Straight sex videos are the best sellers of all, closely followed by ones on spanking. Even if you don't feel like visiting the red-light area, you can obtain a sight of the sort of material available by looking at *The Electronic Tabernacle* on the top floor of the Erotic Museum. Twelve films play simultaneously throughout the day. Eleven of these are sex films; the twelfth is just a TV pop music channel that provides the sound. Some of the films carry English subtitles to leave you in no doubt about what's going on. I thought about taking a photo of this electronic marvel, but realised that the film developers would be in trouble if they processed my slides. At least half the screens contained erections – a sight that the legal system in Britain still denies to women in its photographed form. Fortunately it's harder to legislate against what we can see in the flesh. As you watch all the screens, your attention is taken by one, then transfers to another. The actors seem to be more health-conscious than Danish prostitutes – there are plenty of condoms used in these films. My favourite of the screens – the one my eyes kept returning to, was playing the pornographic version of Snow White. It's a well-drawn, amusing adult animation – the heroine services dwarfs with pricks like toadstools, two or three at a time, then hangs them up on her washing-line when they're too shagged out for any more. Walt Disney must be turning in his grave.

Shops also contain a wide range of sex aids and dolls, including the high-class ones built to withstand men of up to 275 pounds (what a vision!). The price range is from £65 to £150, depending on the inclusion of extras like vibrating vaginas, soft pubic hair, squirting breasts and moveable eyes. The most expensive, *Cleopatra*, boasts that she's made of "extra thick rubber vinyl for a long-lasting relationship". Some have a fourth orifice like a wound between the tits – "feed your penis to my sex hungry breasts". There is also a perfumed blow-up *Teenage Standing Doll* with an open mouth for £22. For those who're hard up and only feel they need the lower half of a woman, that's available too in blow-up form for just under £10. Sex organs alone are much more expensive. The female variety comes boxed with a vibrator for just under £50, or £65, if you feel you need two working orifices. Vaginas are modelled realistically and include tatty black pubic hair cut short enough not to get in the way or interfere with visibility.

Shops also stock a large variety of vibrators and dildoes for both men and women. Prices start from about £9. The fullest variety can again be seen, in the Erotic Museum. *Dildo World* is the case all the tourists like to stop and stare at. Most of the aids have pet names – *Travelling Companion, Maiden Comforter, Pink Surprise, Anal-finger without nail*, etc. A label on each gives the date of its invention and the number of copies made. Everyone is riveted by a black dildo so huge that it looks too big to fit anyone I can imagine. It seems like the stuff of fantasies until you read in the records section of the museum about Nellie Dobbs who had eighty-four Victorian pennies put in her fanny at a party in 1851.

The Erotic Museum was the first of its kind. I think every city should have one that mirrors that country's sexuality. The section on prostitution in Copenhagen is small but interesting. The rest of the collection's devoted to erotic art, films, humorous "erotoboxes", life-size tableaux vivants, sex aids, a cinema and postcards from several decades, etc. I was interested to find that cards from the Fifties and Sixties looked the least erotic, while both earlier and later black and white photography seemed much more able to convey the beauty or sensuality of its subjects. Perhaps too much has been covered in one museum. It's a brave attempt though. A large proportion of the visitors seems to be tourists – everyone from students to ancient couples. You can fill in a questionnaire before you leave, in return for a free postcard. The questions are a little worthy: "Did your visit teach you something about the history of eroticism?" etc. Amusing answers could be devised to most of them. Personally, I think the only thing the museum lacks is couches where desires created by the Electronic Tabernacle et al. could be consummated.

Apart from the more visual exhibits, there are sections on men and women who were famous in erotic history. There's the forgotten Leopold Von Sacher-Masoch who invented Masochism, and Dr. Statz who went round the world measuring women's bodies using the "Master Race" as a norm to quantify them by. Unfortunately, some of the information in the museum is a little shoddy. Research sources are rarely quoted in the sections of records and famous people's sex lives. I'd love to know what ancient writer, for instance, tells us that Cleopatra fellated a thousand men in a night.

The true-life story I feel more inclined to believe is that of Hans Christian Andersen who sang soprano and never had anyone of either sex. I was surprised that Copenhagen had yielded no life-size dolls in the shape of Little Mermaids. The Danish enthusiasm for fairy tales and amusement parks is well known. Their Tivoli Gardens was the forerunner of Disneyworld. It contains a Wax museum set up by Louis (i.e. Monsieur) Tussaud. Then there's Legoland…Adult Danes, it seems, continue to play with plastic bits and pieces as they get older. In a city where even the call girls must be "funny", every window in the red-light area has a similar streak of comedy. I liked particularly the male dummy dressed in a rubber mac who had keeled over drunkenly amongst a pile of enemas and bondage equipment. Fairy lights twinkled merrily round the glass and someone had propped an old bike against the window. Some comedy is more conscious. Several shops sell blow-up dolls in the shape of pigs. What else would you expect in the land of bacon? I asked the manager of one shop just what sort of man would invest in a plastic pig for his nights of passion. He admitted that, though his pigs looked good in the window-display, no one had bought one – yet.

# Berlin

FOR THE ENGLISH, Berlin is laden with romantic imagery from Sally Bowles and *Cabaret* to all those hundreds of nameless films about escapes through, over or under the Wall. The night the Wall finally came down I was giving a reading in Cambridge. The students were so excited that a whole bunch of them decided to pick up traps and rush across to see it all for themselves. William Cash was my student host. He has since gone on to become a well-known journalist. That night, he planned to drive to Shropshire and back in order to retrieve his passport and join the general exodus. Perhaps "Where were you when the Wall came down?" is the British equivalent of the American Kennedy question. I'll certainly always remember that night.

In 1992, I met a Berliner over in Israel. He told me that since the Wall had come down, the East had become "one great red-light district". That sounded interesting and I determined to visit Berlin as well as that much more obvious centre of Teutonic sex culture, Hamburg.

When I went to Berlin, I found a very different story. While the East has a higher crime rate than the rest, most of the prostitution has been moved, or moved itself to the West. There's just one street left for kerb-crawlers in the East – *Oranienburger Strasse*, near *Marx Engels Platz*. A casual day-time stroll around, going east from *Friedrichs Strasse*, will show you only too plainly why the East is no longer an ideal area for street prostitution. In Berlin's attempts to tear out all evidence of the infamous Wall's existence, every road adjacent to that area contains massive craters and building sites fenced off the wire mesh. It's a nightmare to walk round these parts, and even more of a nightmare to kerb-crawl.

While all forms of prostitution are legal in Germany, the police do like to keep an eye on things. Areas are designated by mutual agreement. There's a tiny seedy pocket by the old Charlottenburg station – a video sex-shop, the *Evi Club* upstairs in a hotel and the *Blauer Engel* at the bottom of *Kaiser Friedrich Strasse*. The latter certainly doesn't conjure up visions of Marlene Dietrich. Currently though, *Kurfürsten Strasse* and *Kurfürstendamm* are the main prostitution streets in the West with the greatest number of girls congregating near the corner of *Genthiner Strasse*. These roads are on the border between the *Tiergarten* and *Schöneberg* areas. *Strasse des 17 Juni* which runs across the *Tiergarten* is also known for a kerb-crawling scene.

Schöneberg is one of the most expensive and pleasantest areas of Berlin. It's known for its gay scene. There are several gay bars along *Welser Strasse, Fugger Strasse* and *Motz Strasse: Kitchen, Krast* (which means "gaol") *Tom's* and also a gay disco, *Connection Berlin.* The latter was formerly a transvestite cabaret.

While Munich has the exotic gay Mardi Gras carnival that attracts the odd English visitor too, for year-round tolerance to gays, Berlin takes the prize. It's an easy place to live in if you're gay. I even saw a lesbian magazine advertised on the tube trains there. A much funnier bill posted along the streets showed the lower halves of several young men in snowy Persil-white boxer shorts. It was advertising a "Gay Tea Dance".

The gay scene is primarily amateur. I didn't see a single gay or transvestite prostitute on the streets. Who need pay for it, anyway, with all the gay picking-up going on? Any gay pro – and they are few and far between – will put his name and number in the *Berliner Zeitung* which carries a small personal column. The day I bought a copy, there were only elderly heterosexuals seeking soul mates plus a discreetly-worded ad for *Boys Only Boys Club* which seems to be the local gay chat line.

Once upon a time Berlin was known for its travesty shows. While there are still a few of these shows left as a kind of tourist attraction, they seem to be divorced from the sex scene. There will always be some escorts attached to a night club, anywhere in the world, but Berlin's prostitution is primarily a street scene according to one of the women who works for HYDRA, the newly-formed prostitutes' union. The letters of the word HYDRA are not an acronym. The name was chosen for its shock value – they wanted to be compared with the Greek monster. HYDRA seeks new rights for prostitutes – a social services card that would entitle them to various benefits.

Although prostitution's legal, the German police are curiously unhelpful when girls suffer violence from their clients. The police are a very obvious presence on the streets. Two of them came up and asked me what exactly I was doing while I was interviewing a prostitute with the help of a German friend. Most of these prostitutes are drug-users intent on earning enough money to fund their habit. One of those I talked to used to go home as soon as she'd made enough money – the 300 or 400 marks she needed (£120 to £160) per day. Another said that she serviced four or five men a night. The majority of the women working the street seem to be in their twenties. I only saw one middle-aged one. There didn't seem to be any that looked under-age, though one told me that she'd started at twelve.

Sex is priced at about 50 DM (£22) for a blowjob. Fucking is slightly more at 60 DM and both together, 70 DM. Half an hour in a room would be 100 DM (£45). A few hours or a whole night would be several times that. Sex more often takes place quickly in a car up some dark street. Both the prostitutes I talked to at length preferred German clients. Foreigners didn't want to use condoms, one complained. The other said that they were violent or aggressive, the Russians being worst in that respect. The German punters weren't always an easy trick, either. Both girls said there were many perverts among them. The first complained of sadomasochists, the second that she'd been asked to drink pee and eat shit.

Street walking in Berlin is certainly no picnic. First there's the severe cold with winds blowing in from the East. Those who don't go home, or off to get their fix, might work from ten at night through to six in the morning. Most of the prostitutes aren't really dressed for the cold. The only concession to the weather's the odd leather jacket, or a thin pair of trousers. The difficulty with gearing your life towards car sex is that clothes that are quickly undoable, or raisable, are no real protection against winter weather. There is also another little, or rather large, problem. Berlin happens to be the dog-shit capital of Europe. The hounds in the West are of course better fed than those in the East. You can see the evidence of high-life on muesli, pumpernickel and every type of *Wurst* on every pavement. All the most sensible prostitutes stand on the road instead.

For those that prefer an utterly safe sex experience there are many sex shops to choose from. Several run non-stop programmes of videos. The *ABC Kino* specialises in short gay ones. *Kurfürstendamm* is the best street for peep shows, but there's a scattering of them in sex shops throughout the city. The machines are worked with 1, 2 and 5 DM coins. Few of the machines say how many you would need to see a short film or a live striptease. The only one with more complete instructions specified 8 DM to start a film. If you came in with a sack of change you could stay there all day and night. Each shop boasts of the array of films on offer. One of the largest shops, *Sexyland* on the corner of *Martin Luther Strasse*, boasts a programme of 96 different videos and has instructions in eight languages. For 30 DM (£13) you can see a live striptease from a booth. The stripper, a large black woman in a gold and black wrap, emerged to buy herself a tin of coke from the machine. One of the features of German sex-shops is that you can buy yourself a soft drink, a coffee, a bar of chocolate, or a bag of munchies and take it in with you while you view the videos – a very civilised custom. It stops the punters fainting from hunger while they romp from channel to channel.

*Sexyland* also contains a mini-supermarket for sex toys. You can go round and fill up a plastic basket with magazines, dildoes, bondage gear and dolls. The latter come in several varieties that might be difficult to obtain outside Germany. There are several types of hermaphrodite (I've only seen anything similar in Tel Aviv). *TV Temptation* and *Lusty Bisexual Sweetheart* (a snip at 86 DM – £36) who are both female apart from the vibrating penis protruding from his/her latex panties. There is also *Talking Lora* who "moans and groans and begs for more", a *Teenage Bending Doll* (perfumed), *School Girl* and *Zena Fulsom* who sports huge tits. Last but definitely not least, there's *Big Babe*. Even the picture on her box is a seriously gruesome sight. It's obviously a photo of a real woman rather than a doll, four hundred pounds of quivering cellulite. She'd have been too much for Rubens, but the *Sunday Sport* would probably love her.

# Los Angeles

THERE'S MORE THAN one red light district in Los Angeles these days. While the rich will go to the likes of Heidi Fleiss to procure girls, those who would rather take their chances on the street opt for Sunset Boulevard, or, at the lower end, Main Street. Bottom of the barrel is Fifth Union where Fifth and Union Street intersect. At night, prostitutes, almost always transvestites, service truckers with a quick blowjob. The area's empty in daylight hours except for the huge trucks driving through. I'm told that the truckers haven't yet realised that the "girls" who service them are men. A friend who was showing me the local sights thought about asking the truckers to see if this theory was right, but I discouraged him. I was inclined to think that a big macho bloke driving a vehicle the size of the pursuing one in Duel might not take kindly to someone who pointed out he'd just stuck his cock in the mouth of another man, albeit one who looked every inch a lady.

The area is full of warehouses and few people actually live there. Those who do are either black or Hispanic. Fifth Street is next to the rich developer suburb known as Bunker Hill. From time to time the police tidy that area, moving the homeless along to Fifth.

Main Street, nearby, is the Hispanic red-light area. I was in a heavy old Mustang with old-fashioned enough doors to be more jack-proof than a modern hire-car. Both there and on Fifth there's a danger of being car-jacked. Once you go into this area and soak up its atmosphere, suddenly everything about the LA riots falls into place. I went there with two male friends, both big enough to look like ample protection, but a local said: "They'd take on the three of you." We had decided to park and chance a swift walk along Main Street. Steve, a homeless Jew, offered to be our guide. We were safer with a local man who knew the street. He concocted a cover story for us. We were Christians from out of town taking a look at the area's problems to report to some churches that were starting a charity for the homeless. He had little use, he told us, for the Christian missions in the area. The Midnight Mission, he claimed, always said: "Come back in the morning!" and Union Rescue was little better. He pointed out the doormen: "Built like gorillas". The last thing a hopeless, helpless, homeless man wanted was to be chucked out by people like that. He was a former addict himself and maintained that the missions needed to be run in a more flexible way with fewer rules and more compassion. He had been working for a charity called Single Room Occupancy but lost his job after being hospitalised with food poisoning. These days he eked out a living on the streets selling flowers off a stall and washing the odd windscreen – that was how he had met us. This way he made enough to cover his food and, if he was lucky, eighteen dollars, the price of a night in "Cockroach Hotel".

Single Room Occupancy run by the Community Rehabilitation Association was a charity aimed at getting addicts and the homeless into bed sit accommodation and off the streets. Steve believed that there were fundamental misunderstandings of what was necessary. As an ex-addict himself he knew that people needed the support of a community rather than to be given a bed-sit with no back up help. Worse still, the building intended for the homeless had not been finished. He had protested all along the way and been labelled an awkward customer. His charity, and all the others that were started to deal with the area's problems were purely political gestures, he felt. He pointed me to a free newspaper that could be picked up from a stand nearby. *Los Angeles Downtown News* contains a staggering cosmeticisation of the situation. Its cover shows a picture of a smug businessman who has obviously never suffered a day's hardship in his life. He is the president of a new music centre adjacent to the area. Other topics covered are Lunch Hour Workouts and Dim Sum. I can't find a line in the paper that seems to fit the atmosphere I had walked through. There is certainly nothing that addresses any of the screamingly obvious problems in the real downtown Los Angeles.

The prostitutes of Main Street are known as *Comfort Ladies*. There are between thirty and forty of them. They are well organised and discreet. They take clients to the local hotels, most of which are full of cockroaches. *Comfort Ladies* are mostly in their thirties, short stout and ugly. They all dress in black and have pot-bellies. They are also known as *Toilet Bowl Women*. The client usually follows them down the street for discretion's sake. There are no pimps. They charge anything from twenty to forty dollars for straight sex (£13 to £26) and are health-conscious enough to use condoms. Cockroach-ridden hotels are eighteen dollars for the night and can sometimes be had for less by the half-hour. Saturdays and Sundays are the prostitutes' best working days. The police mostly turn a blind eye.

Some of the local beer bars also have prostitutes known as *straw-berries*. *Strawberries* are anybody's for a helping of rock cocaine which is worth 4 or 5 dollars. Heroin sells for 10. *Strawberries* can't afford condoms and couldn't care less about their health or anybody else's. The authorities attempt some control on the liquor stores – some have been closed down – but everything else is wildly out of hand. The drug dealing on Main Street is open and obvious. San Julian, round the corner, is wall-to-wall drug-dealers. Muggings and car-jackings are frequent occurrences. Any non-local, especially a non-Hispanic stranger is a fair target. There's a large wire fence with a strip of barbed wire across the top that's known as *The Jack-up Fence*. People are mugged against it – lifted and hooked up on the top. At other times strangers are followed and mugged, round a corner, just out of the area. The missions have made no inroads on crime or drugs. There's a lack of human inter-change between their workers and those who actually live on the streets. One of the missions regularly turns a sprinkler system on any homeless unfortunate enough to lean against its walls.

Main Street also has a couple of sex cinemas, *Regent Theatre* and *Main Theatre*, and a special bar for homosexuals. The gay scene here is mostly amateur. I was allowed a peep into the all-male *Score Bar* at the junction of Fourth and Main Street in my assumed role of Christian investigator. It was early Sunday evening, but already it was full of loving Hispanic boys hugging each other affectionately. The whole contents of the bar looked locked into one embrace.

The other main area of street prostitution is on Sunset Boulevard at the Hollywood end. The hookers are young and pretty – late teens or early twenties. They wear obvious clothes – mostly micro-skirts or shorts, leather jackets and high heels. Everyone seems to be dressed in black, white or orange. The girls in white or orange stand out like cyclists' arm bands in the night. Straight sex is not generally on offer with the American fear of AIDS. The girls get by with safer acts – a blowjob with a condom costs 20 dollars. It's mostly tourists who use them and the act's done in the man's car up a side street. In contrast to Main Street the police are a heavy and obvious presence. They are known for setting up entrapment situations, a fact that means that most of the prostitutes are not willing to talk to journalists. Only a young black girl was willing to give me any answers. It's often said that prostitutes must have eyes in their

backsides to keep out of trouble. The Los Angeles girls are unusu-
ally watchful even by prostitute standards. My two escorts and
myself had parked a block away. One of them sauntered by hoping
to be solicited. The girl he loitered near asked him his make of car
before she would get down to business. He mentioned another type
and she walked off. She had seen the three of us driving by five minutes before and observed the car colour and make. The prostitutes
look out for each other and shout down the road if they see any
police coming. Occasionally, the police do catch up with one
though. I saw one girl who was obviously under-age being stopped
and asked for her ID. She flirted with the two policemen: "You guys
were doing Vice yesterday…" She looked about fourteen and had
no ID. She avoided being picked up by walking away quickly and
darting up a side street.

There's also some drug dealing on Sunset Boulevard – mostly at
the Los Angeles end. One of the curious sights, late at night, is the
fact that every public phone is occupied by a fast-talking man. You
overhear phrases like: "Have we got a deal?" Some of the prostitutes
know the men and chat in passing.

I talked to the policemen who had just let the young prostitute
get away. I took a card from one of them – and yes, Hollywood
detectives do have business cards. He thought I could ring his boss
at the department and ask a few questions. In the end it proved
more difficult. He told me to ring that night to set up an appointment for the following morning. I rang the number and the recep-
tionist told me that all the vice squad were out for the night. She
gave me another number to ring. I did so, explaining my mission,
and was told that it was entirely the wrong department and no one
from vice would be there in the morning. I rang the former number. Once I re-explained my project the phone was put down.

Punters in Los Angeles who want slightly more than a blowjob
must go to a masseuse or masseur. There are also masseurs for
women. Their prices start at 65 dollars. Prices for male customers
start at about 75. Some of the masseuses are also clairvoyants. The
best places to find advertisements for these are in free papers like
*LA Village View*, *Los Angeles Reader* or *LA X…Press*. There is also
*Hollywood Playdates*, "an adult newspaper for men, women and couples 18 and over". It's sold from boxes on the streets late at night.
It's good value at a dollar for the sort of pictures that only appear in
glossy mags on our newsagents' top shelves at several times the

price. It's also the best place to find contact numbers for telephone sex.

Some of the free papers are available in *Little Frida's*, an excellent coffee shop on the Santa Monica Boulevard. Most of its clientele is lesbian. The café's named after the Mexican painter, Frida Kahlo, and a picture of her hangs on the wall. Little Frida's also stocks free gay contact and information magazines – *Spunk* and *Planet Homo* for men and *Female FYI* for women. Some of the local discos advertise parties with a sexual theme. If you go to one party you are handed a flyer about the next – "Skin Parlor with live demos hosted by the Rubber Mistress". *Spunk* advertises a *Mile High Club* that has parties aboard a jet to New York. There is also rumoured to be an exclusive gay orgy club in Hollywood with rich and influential members who have all passed an HIV test before being allowed to join.

Until recently one of the best disco nights out could be had at *Club Fuck*, but the police closed it down. Parties always included a live act. The party before the closure had involved a man with pierced nipples threading Christmas tree lights through them, then lighting up. *Club Fuck*'s place has been taken by the weekly *Sin-a-matic* disco, opposite the Lee Strasberg Theatre Institute. It has an attractively decadent show – two black devils dressed in codpieces, horns, white socks and Doc Martens and two women in flower-covered leotards and head-dresses. Their act contained some simulated but clothed fucking and a lot of energetic dancing. One of the male devils ate bunch after bunch of grapes and offered them to the audience. He had the high bottom and protuberant stomach you see in some African tribes – or perhaps he just ate too much fruit! The dancers are not, as you might expect, would-be actors. They are simply those who want to dance the night away and get paid 75 dollars at the same time. The club is full of attractive people of all sexes, some of them exotically dressed. One man wore just a leather pinafore. Another had a black patent plastic dress with pink chiffon sleeves and vast silicone implants. He'd just had them done and all his friends were admiring his cleavage. The music is Techno. It sounds like a mixture of New Age Music with a heavy African drumbeat that drowns the words of the songs. The air is scented with strawberry and vanilla. Slides are projected on one side wall. As a former art history student I found them riveting – pictures from the Villa of the Mysteries at Pompeii, satyrs from Greek vases, Archimboldo's faces made of fruit, Pan figures, corn goddesses, huge flowers by Georgia O'Keefe, Orpheus, a goat skull, Leda and the Swan – a true celebration of everything pagan. The disco is particularly popular with Russians and generally a good pick-up point for people of every sexual orientation.

The other well-known pick-up point is *Boystown* – part of the Santa Monica Boulevard. It's essentially an amateur area. While some prostitution goes on there, there's no fixed price. It's all done by mutual agreement.

Scattered across Hollywood and Los Angeles there are also a number of strip shows and sex shops. The shows are just basic striptease with the odd table dance. One of the oldest establishments is the *Century Nude Theatre*, near the airport. It charges 10 dollars entry. There's no alcohol inside, only vitamin drinks. The shop next door charges men 50 cents for entry, while women are allowed in free. Most of its custom comes from tourists who come from stricter countries to buy videos with titles like *Harry Horndog, Fat Fuckers, Blame it on Bambi, Black Dicks White Chicks* and *Freaks of Nature*. The cover of the latter shows a man with two cocks being sucked off. Every country likes different titles of video, different dolls and different books. Americans seem to be great readers judging by the quantity of books stocked: *Raunchy Reporter, Busty Trailblazer,* and *Rodeo Romance…* As in Germany, the *Big Babe* doll is freely available together with *Disco Doll* (red-haired), *Greek Girl, Slave Girl, Wayne Doll* "a real man about town" and *Private Secretary*. But, above all, the main speciality of Los Angeles Sex shops is flavoured lubricants. These come in about as many varieties and similar flavours as American ice creams and muffins. It's hard to know what to choose when confronted with rows of *Blueberry Blintz, Peppermint Candy, Body Butter, Banana Split, Banana Daiquiri, Pina Colada, Passion Fruit* or *Spicy Orange*. Los Angeles specialised in these creams long before other parts of the world. Americans have a strongly oral orientation. An Irish poet once told me a splendid story. His friend had just been to LA and seen all these products. "Well, Seamus, so what did you bring back?" the less-travelled poet asked. "I didn't buy any for my wife," the other replied. "They were out of smoky bacon-flavoured." Prices of lubricants start at just under six dollars. The real rip-off is the aerosols of cream which are more expensive – considerably more so than an ordinary aerosol of cream from the average supermarket.

The best sex-shop in Los Angeles is the *Pleasure Chest* along the

Santa Monica Boulevard. It's the only shop where you'll see more women customers than men – probably because of the vast array of cunnilingual creams and dominatrix gear. For the severely sado-masochistic, tractor chain, sold by the yard, is available, labelled with a government warning: "Not to be used for overhead lifting. Do not exceed working load limit." Other gentler fetishes are also catered for with kits like: *Shave your Honey* which contains shaving cream, a razor, aftershave gel, finishing powder, a white feather and a black G-string, or *The Human Bonbon Kit* which contains a pound of chocolate, a paint brush, a jar of cherries, a package of peanuts and a "drop cloth" whatever that is. For the less imaginative there are also plenty of condoms with butch names like *Trojan, Trojan Magnum, Excalibur, Sheik* or *Ramsses*. The assistants are very helpful and discuss their products lovingly: " It'll fit snug on you. It won't move on you" they tell the bondage customers as they buy the *Missionary Pleasure Sling, Lust Loops* or *Cumfy Cuffs.* " Everyone is allowed to browse too, like the Arab who was happily testing a cat o' nine tails on his hand. Unlike other American shopkeepers these assistants are tactful when you buy something and don't say, "Have a nice day!" or, worse still, "Have a nice night!"

# Budapest

IN RECENT YEARS, the Russian Mafia has become entrenched in the club scene in Budapest. Many prostitutes operate from or near clubs. The management takes a cut. Others work by all-night supermarkets. The thing that both types of establishment have in common is a series of running lights round the doors or windows. Clubs will attract a mixture of locals and tourists. Many club names are aimed at the international market, e.g. Miami, Caligula, Bar Sixty Nine, Sweet Mick and Paradiso. A club with a Hungarian name, Rozsaszin Cica advertises more exotic acts – Akrobat , Lesbos, etc. It is just round the corner from the National Theatre.

The Halló topless bar had a coupon offering free entry in a local tourist brochure. Free entry, I found when I got there, was confined to blokes. I argued, but the doorman was a lot bigger than I was… I was told by those who had visited the Halló and similar establishments that they were simply strip joints with prostitutes in attendance. Prostitution is illegal, but it goes on. The prices are not cheap for fairly ordinary-looking girls. They are usually about 150 DM for straight sex (£67). Deutschmarks and hard currency are much preferred to forints.

Most clubs operate from eight or so in the evening until the small hours. Those who want twenty-four hour prostitution go to Rákoczi Tér (Square). It's next to a food market that is open by day. There's a small sordid park in the middle. At night it's ill lit and sinister. Rubbish from the market blows about the street. Men hang about with the women – pimps, clients or friends – it's not always easy to tell.

After talking with a few young Rumanian and Russian would-be punters across the main road, I went over and tried to get acquainted with the prostitutes. One of them, "Anna", knew a little English. One of the men standing near her knew a little more. Anna was short and fat with a round permanently smiling face. She had a very heavy bosom and hennaed hair. The first prices she quoted for different types of sex were in Deutschmarks. She always used condoms and had no trouble from the police. She specialised in anal sex for 50 DM and group sex for 200. By the end of the night, I was able to imagine quite what group sex might involve for the poor client.

The group huddled closely round me as I asked questions.

Everybody seemed friendly and jokey, language difficulties permitting, that is until I noticed that my bag was open. I had several things on me that I shouldn't and wouldn't have taken into such an area under normal circumstances, but I was in Budapest, wearing two hats as it were. Officially, I was reviewing the spring music festival for one of the daily newspapers. I had been out all day sightseeing and going to concerts, and had not had time to return to my hotel either in the afternoon, or after Beethoven's *Missa Solemnis*.

I went back to the main road to check what was missing. At that stage it was just some travellers' cheques. While I was looking in my bag a woman came up and asked if I was in trouble. I said that some travellers' cheques had been stolen. She then advised me to look and see if my passport was okay. Foolishly, I said that it was still there. In saying that I became a marked woman. The new arrival spoke slightly better English than the prostitute I had been talking to. As she had come from the main road I didn't immediately associate her with being one of that group. She might just have been a local. She was dumpy and middle-aged with short, light brown hair and a grey shell suit. She offered to ask the group to give my travellers' cheques back to avoid further trouble. I waited for a long while and then she returned. They would give them back, she said, just round the corner in a hotel. A small group of four detached themselves and joined the woman. We went to the bottom corner of the square, opposite a Chinese restaurant. By then, seeing no hotel, I was beginning to feel distinctly uneasy. There were now just two men and two women with me. The middle-aged woman showed me a crumpled handful of papers which might, or might not, have been my travellers' cheques. They had been taken out of the passport holder they'd been in. They wanted money for them, she said. I offered a small reward in forints. It wasn't worth more to me, because I knew I could get them replaced, eventually. A much larger sum was demanded. I said I was going. But the first woman gripped my upper arm tightly and the four pushed me further along the road and further away from any possible help. I began to scream and scream and scream. It seemed my only hope. One of the four began to hit me. I was hemmed in by two on either side, so I could not attempt to run for it. Fortunately, it was the smallest of the group that punched me. If the others had joined in, I wouldn't have been able to walk away from the incident. The two prostitutes were short but bulky and could probably have packed quite a punch if they put their weight into it. The other man was medium height and quite strongly built. He certainly could have inflicted some damage. But it was the tiny pimp or sneak thief who was elected to do the hitting. At moments of danger time slows down immensely. While still standing there screaming, I observed the man who was hitting me. I had first seen his sort before on the streets of Palermo. It's a physical type that turns up in the slummiest parts of major cities around the world. You know, just by looking at them, that such boy-men or men-boys have grown up on the streets in an amoral life of hardship. They are always small and weak in build, five feet or less in height, with a grey skin and beady watchful eyes that take in at a glance every item that might be worth stealing. I did not hit back. If the violence had become a free-for-all, I would have been a lot worse off. The small man punched me five times before he could pull my bag away. I had held on, suddenly becoming conscious of everything I did not want to lose in the way of bits of make-up and my address book. As the shoulder strap of my bag broke, a few items fell on the ground and I was able to recover these later. The thief ran one direction and his friends in the other. Probably they had arranged to meet up later to share out the goods.

I walked to the nearest bar and found someone who spoke some English. The bar man telephoned the police and offered me a drink while I waited. Knowing I could not pay I opted for water instead. The police were there soon. We drove past the square, but most of the prostitutes had scattered.

An interpreter had to be called in so that I could make a full statement. Veronika came from her sickbed, a fluey cold, and I was apologetic. She said she did not mind though. She'd get good overtime for a night call, which was just what she needed as she was saving for a trip to Paris to see her daughter.

The statement took hours. It was the early hours of the Bank Holiday after Easter Sunday. I was due to leave the next day and needed a "protocol" to get a new passport.

Under Hungarian law, hitting someone to take his or her money is an entirely different matter from just opening a handbag. If I were to pursue the assault charge I'd need to wait around days and have a medical examination that morning. I knew there'd be nothing to show at this stage. I'd been wearing a thick coat over a leather jacket and it had absorbed most of the punches, which had all been to the arms or shoulders. In a few days' time I would have a bruise, but that was all. By then, I would be out of Hungary. I dropped the assault charge and went for the lesser one of theft.

By four in the morning the officer who was writing the statement was so sick of it all that he determined to wind things up. He'd had enough of my detailed descriptions and decided to print it all out then and there. Only two of the group were described. The little man was made slightly more normal in height and both were described as Gypsies, not Hungarians. I insisted this description was removed. While the stronger man of the four might have been one, I don't believe that any of the others were. The police like to assume that all the prostitution and thefts are the work of Gypsies. I was told that none of them were ever caught, so that it did not matter if all four descriptions were not included. While the police were helpful and courteous enough, there was a flaw in their system of justice. The man who wrote my statement put down what he wanted to believe rather than the whole truth. I have a feeling that much the same would happen here to a foreign journalist mugged in London's equivalent nightspot, King's Cross.

After spending hours cancelling credit cards and getting money from American Express, I tried to get a passport from the British Embassy. I was to feel even more robbed by their answer. A Bank Holiday call-out would cost £200. On normal days I could have a new temporary passport for £5. Embassy staff are also not trained in basic courtesies like "Are you all right? Were you hurt?" etc.

I had offered to drive round with the police to pick out the thieves. I remembered their faces well. But, I was told the police did not have the time. It's a pity they don't drive by Rákoczi Tér more often; it might prove a slight deterrent. I had also asked to be driven back via there so that I could perhaps recover anything else that had been dropped. I did find one or two more small items of make-up, lipstick, etc. My mirror also lay on the ground undamaged. The police hurried me home at this stage. I returned in the day on foot for a quick search of the local bins in case the mugger had ditched my handbag nearby, but I wasn't lucky. There were still prostitutes at work in the area, but not the ones of the night before.

I have often wandered who got my passport in the end. I hope it was someone unfortunate rather than a real criminal. Somewhere there was an Eastern European Fiona Pitt-Kethley carrying my identity until 1996. I wandered also what the going rate for a passport was? I was to find out months later when I sat next to a man on a coach to Krakow. He was in the shady business of "Import Export" and had plans to be a millionaire by the age of 25. Passports in Eastern Europe currently went at £4,000, he claimed. That's certainly worth entrapping and mugging a tourist for, and could well be a nice sideline to "group sex".

# Hong Kong and Macau

IF TOURISTS, especially male tourists, ask for a red-light area in Hong Kong, they are immediately directed to cross by the Star Ferry to Wanchai. Lockhart Street is lined with dozens of drinking joints where a young sailor can spend a week's pay or more only too easily – *Club Superstar, Club Cheeky, Club Carnival, Club Hot Legs, Club Venus, Club Pussy Cat, The Panda*, etc. – the list is endless. I visited the *New Popeye Club*. There was a pretty Filipino girl dancing. Dancers usually wear underwear or cutaway leotards, and spiked heels. The one before me had heavily-laddered black stockings and a jewelled leotard. Occasionally she pulled a tit out or massaged her pussy to egg on the men at the bar. There were three men sitting there. They were in their late teens or early twenties and probably sailors. Even to my unpractised eyes they had that slightly glazed "Please rob me!" expression in their eyes. Mostly bar girls only go-go dance and bare the odd tit as the night goes on. Occasionally if interest needs to be stimulated, they press their genitals against a potential customer's nose, or simulate a little cunnilingus with one of the other dancers. There are usually two or three in a bar. They are almost always Filipino or Thai.

There are many far cheaper places to have sex in the world. *The New Popeye* is considered one of the straighter establishments in that it displays the prices of its drinks – *Sweet Pea, Olive Oyl* and *Popeye* – at 110, 220 and 330 Hong Kong dollars (£11, £22, £33). These are mostly fruit juices with perhaps a dash of spirits if you're lucky. The young sucker will be expected to buy himself and the hostess a couple of drinks apiece before the price of a bar fine is even discussed. The bar fine which lets a girl off for long enough to find a hotel where she will spend only as long as it takes for the man to come, or a maximum of half an hour, is anything from one to three thousand Hong Kong dollars (£100 to £300), depending on the club. The next payment is for the hotel. Hotel Berkeley is one of those most commonly used. It lets rooms by the half-hour. Hotel prices vary from 200 to 600 (£20 to £60) of which the girl will get back £5 in commission. Thus, it's near impossible for clients to spend less than £250 for what is no more than a very quick fuck with a relatively ordinary hostess in a cheap hotel.

A westerner in search of commercial sex who knows Hong Kong

better than the young sailors who turn up on Lockhart Street can find himself a more reasonably priced deal in another part of town. There's a scattering of clubs in the Kowloon area, *Red Lips* in Lock Road, for instance. In this sort of club the drinks are usually around £5 and bar fines are £50 or so with the price of a cheap hotel on top. Alternatively, Hong Kong residents can get an introduction to a local brothel. Chinese prostitutes are deeply suspicious of western men, and invariably charge them double the local rates. For a Chinese man sex would cost in the region of £5 to £20 depending on the time spent and what was involved. A foreigner is unlikely to get away with paying less than £70. If he becomes a long-term client he might get two girls for that. That's something the locals don't get, or aren't interested in.

I had been corresponding with Don, an academic at Hong Kong University, for years but I had not actually met him. Within a quarter of an hour from our first encounter in the Kowloon Hotel, I was watching him on the job beneath a mirrored ceiling at Madame Kwai's small establishment.

Mirrors are a feature of Hong Kong brothels. The more expensive the brothel the more mirrors it will have. "The more important the client, the more he wants to see himself!" Madame Kwai had been told that I was running a similar establishment to hers in the South of England and wanted to pick up some tips. Don swore that I would never have been allowed inside if she'd known I was a journalist.

The prostitutes were both middle-aged and ordinary looking. One had full breasts and purple nipples. The other was flatter and broader in body. The flatter one fellated Don to get him erect for the job. He kept pleading for a massage. Massage, and sometimes even a facial, is very much part of the eastern sex scene. Chinese prostitutes are also extremely health-conscious. There's a government health ad around – the only English words on it are "MR CONDOM". The commonest local brand name is also in English – *GENTS*. Not only do many prostitutes use a couple of condoms on their clients, but they also go through elaborate rituals of washing them and searching the body hair of westerners. God only knows what they expect to find. Don had plenty of chest hair for them to search. He relayed the odd question to the two girls in Cantonese while the act went on. I was wary of asking too many as I didn't want to spoil his 70 quid's worth. (Madame Kwai had generously allowed me to observe free.) Chinese prostitutes put on a certain show of affection and an obligatory faked orgasm. Don told me he'd begged them not to bother with the latter, but they insisted. It was part of their trade. The girls before me sighed, cooed, oohed, aahed and rolled up their eyes at appropriate moments. The effect of the second girl's "orgasm" was thoroughly spoiled by the other one cleansing herself noisily in the next room. The woman who had been doing the sucking off spat loudly, showered, then started spitting again, hawking coughing and gagging for minutes next door.

For the last few years, Madame Kwai herself had serviced Don until she found a new patron. Now he gets her best girls. He recommended the place, as he'd never caught anything there. There'd be little chance of that with all the condoms in evidence. Madame Kwai was even more particular than her girls. Don swore that she used to put a condom on every finger of a client before he was allowed to touch her. He rather missed her facials. The girls would only do body massage.

Madame Kwai's establishment was tucked away discreetly above a photographer's that specialised in school and family portraits, in Pak Hoi Street off the Nathan Road. The only clue to its identity was the word Apartments in the title. Wherever you see a name like *VIP Apartments* it means that there's a brothel that caters for westerners as well as locals. Truly local brothels can also be found if you know the appropriate Chinese kanji – the sign for a woman that appears in all the notices outside. It looks more like a fish standing on its tail than a woman, but it's worth memorising as it turns up in Japan and Singapore as well. If you find it in red on a yellow neon sign with green letters below, you are at the right place. Occasionally though, colour-blind westerners are misled into a woman's wear establishment that also has the sign for woman as part of its title but isn't in the tell-tale yellow and red. The best streets for a concentration of brothels are *Sham Shui Po* and the aptly named *Fuk Wa*. Prostitutes in these establishments will be Chinese or Thai. The Thai girls are sometimes illegal immigrants.

The younger Chinese girls in the business usually lead a double life. They might be married, or hold down another job. By the time a prostitute is middle-aged in Hong Kong, her attitude is different. Women in this age bracket are often quite open about what they do. By this stage they may be divorced or bringing up a family alone.

Prostitution might pay a son's or daughter's university fees.

It's fashionable in Hong Kong to christen yourself with an extra western name or two. In more respectable jobs, men favour Hector or Aloysius, and women, Grace, Agnes, Agatha, Esmeralda, Amy or Jessie. In brothels, girls almost always opt for Susie after Susie Wong. While their real names might be something like Mei-ling, Ying-ling or Siu-li, they will always be Susie to their western clients. They often also have other pet or code names like Ah-Ling. A client like Don, who speaks some Cantonese, will pick-up on these other names as the girls talk to each other. There are a few brothels with a larger quantity of girls that run the place in a more impersonal fashion. You can order up a girl by her number, like the sweet and sour in a Chinese takeaway.

There are a few brothels in the Mong Kok area, which are staffed by younger girls and also seem to have younger clients. There are also working class, purely local establishments. You have to know the address and be Chinese for these. There is no visible sign outside. These are known as fish-bowl stalls. The name comes from a curious metaphor. These establishments sell a quick grope in the dark for £2. The fondling movement is thought to be similar to the movement of fish in a bowl. These establishments are stocked with young girls and mostly appeal to young and poor clients. It's not openly admitted, but presumably they could go on to strike a further bargain with the girls for full sex.

Any drug problem in Hong Kong is separate from prostitution. A prostitute's money is usually used for living expenses and educating her family. There are few pimps in the business. Only occasionally, a girl is run by the doorman that she took on to deal with any troublesome clients. Where there are Madames they, of course, take a share of the profits, often half. They have to pay out heavily to the authorities in order to remain in business. If they don't pay they are raided. Surprisingly, there is little triad involvement in prostitution. Perhaps the money involved just isn't enough. Triads seem far more concerned with the rich jewellers these days.

The chief area for street prostitution is in *Yaumatei*, alongside the wholesale market in Reclamation Street and in the side streets nearby. Prostitutes will ask for £70 but settle for £10 or £15. They are usually the choice of the local schoolboys. Older men tend to prefer brothels. There's a scattering of street prostitution in smarter areas too. It's extremely hard to recognise until you know the rules.

A prostitute is never dressed tartily; her clothes are one grade up in smartness on those of the other people in the area she works. She can also be known in a city where everyone walks fast and does business all the time, by the fact that she is the only person who is loitering without a mobile phone.

There is also prostitution in the provinces near Hong Kong. I took a day trip to Macau. The Portuguese province of Macau is a gambler's paradise. Where there are rich gamblers there have to be women for them to spend it on. The prostitution there is all hotel-centred. I expected it to be a call-girl system, but I was told that it operates chiefly in the saunas. I went in the slightly seedy *Sintra* to investigate. Having got used in Hong Kong to the need for a non-journalistic alibi, I pretended to be a secretary taking a price list for her boss who was about to come there on a business trip. My boss was very keen on saunas and massage, I lied. The main desk pretended ignorance of the hotel sauna's prices. I had to sneak up the back stairs to ask. The sauna was only open in the afternoon, was Gentlemen Only and cost £18 to £25. Curiously, sex in Macau is supposed to be more of a late morning to afternoon affair in such establishments. Probably the evening is kept for serious gambling.

Currently a strange rumour is running through Hong Kong about the economic zone of *Zhuhai*, which is just over the border from Macau. The story runs that there's a brothel full of old women. The workers, it's claimed, are all eighty plus. Don theorised though, that some might be sixty posing as eighty to get work. The rates are supposed to be £10 for sex, £8 for blowjobs or £12 for blowjobs without teeth. The story first reached mass circulation in the pages of *Private Eye*. I have since got my agent to approach his friends there. I also put out feelers via Jung Chang of *Wild Swans* fame. But alas, nobody has come up with the exact address. If they do, I could ask Don to consumer-test the place. He is one of those rare men who appreciate the importance of female wisdom and experience…

# Hamburg

HAMBURG HAS A reputation as one of the most important red light districts in the world. It's a pleasantly drunken city where everyone falls out of tube trains and weaves along the road. Most of the prostitution operates on the roads just off the *Reeperbahn*. The gay section is in *Hein-Hoyerstraße*, with the *Gay Kino* cinema, a gay sexshop and a few camp sailors on the street.

There is much more for the heterosexual in Hamburg. I went round these areas with a former boyfriend. A six foot eight German makes a useful bodyguard and interpreter. There were two areas I could not penetrate as a female, so I went back alone later in the male disguise I'd perfected in Turkey. I hadn't wanted Jürgen to see me in bother boots and no eye make-up.

Jürgen was due to run the Hamburg Marathon next day and I cajoled him into going up to prostitutes in various areas, asking their prices and engaging them in conversation as if he were a prospective customer. In some areas, I lost track of him for so many minutes I wondered if I'd lost him altogether. I sent him first to the *Kontakthof* and *Love Center* . To get into this area you walk down a side road painted with slogans like: *CRAZY SEXY.* The girls are in an underground car park. No other women are allowed inside, although many middle-aged Fraus try to have a look, then stumble out laughing with their husbands who look as if they'd like to stay a bit longer. The girls are young and pretty. Most are dressed in highcut leotards or swimsuits and other scanty sports wear. They charge 50 DM (£22) for 45 minutes of ordinary sex. 100 DM can buy you some abnormality – bondage or a duo, for instance. The girls in this area are probably the prettiest in Hamburg. Jürgen remarked on what good value they were. Those on the street are a little worse in looks and their prices are more varied. Most seem to be in their twenties or thirties. The police drive by on the main road and keep a discreet eye, ready for any trouble.

Across the opposite side of the *Reeperbahn* there are many prostitutes on side streets like the *Erichstraße*. *Herbertstraße*, off *Davidstraße*, contains another men-only area, hidden by barriers at either end. Again, the Fraus try to get in, but are thrown out. I entered in my male guise, later in the evening. It's a street of houses with windows of girls bathed in violet light. All the black girls wear white underwear and the white girls, black. Sex takes place in the apartments above. The prices are the same as those in the car park, but for half an hour rather than forty-five minutes.

Back on *Davidstraße*, one of the girls was "checking" every good-looking young man who goes down the street, dodging in their path like a skilled netball-player. I watched her while Jürgen chatted to another girl. The "Artful Dodger" in front of me noticed my looking back and waiting for him. "Nicole, it's an item," she shouted. Prostitutes often look out for one another.

It was time for Jürgen to go to bed alone. He had a Marathon to run. It was too early for me, so I headed for the sex shows. The Reeperbahn is one of the few places left where you can still see sex on stage. The main sex shows are all sited on the *Große Freiheit* – *the Tanga Club, Tabu Club, The Pattaya Beach Club* (with Thai girls), *the Salambo* and a few other smaller places. *The Salambo* is the best known of the sex theatres and is supposed to put on a more tasteful show. I opted instead for the oldest joint. I think it was the friendly persuasiveness and good English of Charlie, the Nigerian tout, outside the *Tanga Club*.

While the more modern clubs might specialise in Thai girls, the Tanga always provides the odd black and white mixed act. In view of the old large dick theory, it's always a black man and a white girl. Germans, in particular, are supposed to find the idea of sex between different races erotic. *The Tanga's* a small club with a witch ball above a small stage. The maximum seating capacity is twenty-six, but customers come and go. At least half of them are Japanese and are greeted "*Sayonara!*" by the club's boss as they leave. There's no cover charge. Instead, the punter has to buy a minimum of two drinks, beer or coke, for 35 DM (£15). You can make your two drinks last as long as you like. There's no pressure to leave. The acts are slow, so many people stay for a couple of hours. There were supposed to be 26 acts throughout the night. The first few were strippers and fairly ordinary-looking. Some were middle-aged, late forties or fifty. A beefy Malaysian girl with a German body and Asian facial features stripped from short black skirt and jacket with sequin appliqués down to a wide body belt and stockings. Several performers wore wide belts round the middle to hide poor stomach tone. The girls had names like Candy. One of them retired to chat up customers at the bar.

The next performers were a sex act. The lights were dimmed and they lay down on a sheepskin rug. The man did a shoulder-stand to remove his briefs. He was a miserable-looking South American. Many performers come from Chile. His woman partner lay down beside him and started to play with his cock. He took the whole of "I got my thrill on Blueberry Hill!" to get erect. Then he fucked her. She had one leg on his shoulder, the other down. I saw her face more clearly when she turned over and knelt. She wore only high heels and a stomach band to hold her in. The doggy position is very unflattering to all but the flattest of stomachs. Katya had the most truly bored expression I have ever seen in my life while her beau fucked her. For the third go she got on top. The fourth was another doggy near the front row. Katya started chatting to the audience while the Chilean kept up his stroke. In the mean time, a couple of henchmen fixed a swing to the ceiling near the witch ball. The next bout of sex was to James Bond theme tunes. She lay across various men's laps for the fifth fuck and on the bar for the sixth. The last fuck was on the swing, to German Bier Keller music. They swung violently. She faced her partner on his lap. It was the only part I found even faintly erotic. The dour facial expressions hadn't helped the rest. Having tried all the other positions, I couldn't help wondering what doing it on a swing was like. Unfortunately, I haven't been able to persuade anyone to desecrate children's playgrounds.

The best of the strippers was "Miss Susie Wong" of Bangkok, who came on in a side-split red satin dress and put all sorts of somersaults and the splits into her act. She had a slightly humorous expression that certainly was one up on Katya's. Most of the strippers looked partly exotic, Brazilians, Chileans, Thais, etc. Katya came on again and did another simple strip routine, looking as bored and fed-up as ever. Most of the acts were announced in a sentence of German – "*Meinen Damen und Herren*," etc., then English. Eventually, the mixed race act came along – Betty and Roy. Betty sat on a special set like a doll's house with the front off. She was every inch the bored housewife looking for something to do. Eventually, she drummed her fingertips, then picked up the phone: "*Mein Radio ist kaput!*" she complained. Even the non-German-speaking Japanese in the front row knew exactly what was coming. Betty sprayed perfume under her arms and around her fanny before Roy, the black hunk entered to repair her radio and all the rest. She offered him a drink, then got to work sucking his cock and playing with his balls. Roy had an American accent: "Yeh, yeh, around the

second hole, know what I mean?" I assumed anal sex was intended
but she obviously took it that he wanted a finger up his bum. Roy
had a slightly protuberant stomach and could have done with the
loan of Katya's body belt. He kept on his baseball cap and U.S. flag
T-shirt but it didn't cover that stomach in every position. He only
used the tip of his long cock to fuck Betty, lining her up against various items of furniture around the room.

I talked to the middle-aged Hamburgian next door to me. Like
almost all Hamburgians he was pleasantly drunk. He told me I
should have gone to the *Salambo* instead. The girls were prettier.
Pretty girls I can live without. I will never forget Katya's expression.

The sex-shows are closed by day, and the prostitutes are mostly
home sleeping things off. The only place left for the sex tourist is
Hamburg's Erotic Art Museum. It's an incredibly stylish collection.
The museum is in a converted warehouse on *Bernard-Nochtstraße*.
It's near the waterfront and almost next door to a shop selling odd
curios from all over the world – ships in bottles, figureheads, carv-
ings, Balinese puppets and so on. The Museum is packed with drawings, paintings and objects. Some are by famous artists of the past –
Daumier, Cocteau, Grosz, etc. There's a designer exhibition also.
It's currently full of Karin Scholz's work – intricate leather corseted
dummies and carved Art Nouveau furniture, a screen made of
lances, a huge ceramic prick backed by red satin drapes. She has a
sensual and slightly sinister touch for mixing fabrics and styles.
Every floor of the museum is a symphony of textures. Upstairs,
there are more and more watercolours and drawings, some are clev-
erly reflected in mirrors; some are hidden away in cabinets. You
have to pull out trays to look at these. The floors are heavy, uneven,
old wooden planking which adds to the atmosphere. As you go up a
storey, the place gets more solitary and stranger until you come to
the last stairs of all which is blocked by metal cases and a high-
backed chair on which a six foot skein of silver white hair is draped.

Downstairs, back in almost normality, the bookstall sells postcard reproductions of every picture you'd like to send your maiden
aunt or the vicar – everything from hugely endowed devils to sailors
buggering mermaids.

## Books by Fiona Pitt-Kethley

London
Rome
Tower of Glass
Gesta
Sky Ray Lolly
Private Parts
Journeys to the Underworld
The Perfect Man
The Misfortunes of Nigel
The Maiden's Progress
Literary Companion to Sex
Dogs
Too Hot to Handle
The Pan Principle
Literary Companion to Low Life
Cabinet of Curiosities
Double Act
Memo from a Muse

## Books by the Tamworth Press
Red Light Districts of the World
My Schooling: The Autobiography Part One
Baker's Dozen

The Tamworth Press will also be publishing:

Coincidences by James Plaskett